1922
EVERYTHING
*for the*
GARDEN

PETER HENDERSON & CO. 35 AND 37 CORTLANDT ST. NEW YORK

# The Gardener's Bedside Reader

Contributors include Diane Ackerman,
Michael Pollan, Anna Pavord, and more

Kari Cornell, Editor

Voyageur Press

First published in 2008 by Voyageur Press, an imprint of MBI Publishing Company, Galtier Plaza, Suite 200, 380 Jackson Street, St. Paul, MN 55101 USA

Voyageur Press titles are also available at discounts in bulk quantity for industrial or sales-promotional use. For details write to Special Sales Manager at MBI Publishing Company, Galtier Plaza, Suite 200, 380 Jackson Street, St. Paul, MN 55101 USA.

To find out more about our books, join us online at www.voyageurpress.com.

Editor: Kari Cornell
Designer: LeAnn Kuhlmann
Printed in China

*On the front cover:* Burpee's *Offering* catalog, 1917
*On the title page:* Diana Felber's garden, Berkshire Mountains, Massachusetts, *Photograph* © *Jane Booth*

Library of Congress Cataloging-in-Publication Data

The gardener's bedside reader / edited by Kari Cornell.
   p. cm.
 ISBN-13: 978-0-7603-2657-2 (hardbound w/ jacket)
 1. Gardening. 2. Gardens. 3. Gardening—Literary collections. 4. Gardens—Literary collections. I. Cornell, Kari A.
SB455.G353 2008
635—dc22

                              2006023620

# PERMISSIONS

# ACKNOWLEDGMENTS

WHEN THERE IS GARDENING
TO BE DONE,
TWO HEADS ARE BETTER FAR
THEN ONE

As with any book, this one came together because of the work of many dedicated people. I'd like to thank all those who've contributed their stories, photographs, and artwork to the project: William Alexander, Sigrid Arnott, Kathie Bailey, Laura Billings, Jane Booth, Richard Brown, Dixie Cornell, Domenica Di Piazza, Joe Eck, Sydney Eddison, Richard Felber, Jerry Harpur, Dan Hinkley, Jamaica Kincaid, Ann Lovejoy, Tovah Martin, Lee May, Karen Melvin, Henry Mitchell, Lela Nargi, Anna Pavord, Michael Pollan, Vita Sackville-West, Dayle Allen Shockley, and Tasha Tudor and family.

I owe a special thank-you to Suzy Bales, Michael Dregni, Denise Dreher, Josh Leventhal, Elvin McDonald, Bob Payton, and Wayne Winterrowd, who offered new ideas, inspiration, and encouragement throughout the process. And I thank my husband, Brian, who is always my best sounding board, idea man, and friend.

# CONTENTS

*Introduction*
**The Gardener's Bedside Reader**     II

*Chapter 1*     The Perfect Garden     **15**

**Arcadia**
*by Dan Hinkley*     17
**The Garden I Have in My Mind**
*by Jamaica Kincaid*     21
**How Does Your Garden Grow? Any Way You Choose**
*by Henry Mitchell*     27
**Excerpt from *In Your Garden*, February 1948**
*by Vita Sackville-West*     33

*Chapter 2*     The Nitty Gritty     **39**

**Slug Boots: The Northwest's Answer to Pesticides**
*by Ann Lovejoy*     41
**The Delights of Weeding**
*by Suzy Bales*     47
**Growing Regret**
*by Dan Hinkley*     55
**The Vine, or, Garden and Know Thyself**
*by Sigrid Arnott*     63
**Among Heirloom Plants, Always Tread Lightly**
*by Laura Billings*     73

*Chapter 3*     Gardens of Lore                    81

**Tasha Tudor: Springs Eternal**
*by Tovah Martin*                                   83
**The Visitors**
*by Joe Eck*                                        91
**Down the Garden Path**
*by Beverley Nichols*                              99

*Chapter 4*     Vegetable Heaven                    115

**The $64 Tomato**
*by William Alexander*                             117
**Vegetables Again**
*by Lee May*                                       127
**Gardening in the Supermarket**
*by Wayne Winterrowd*                              133

*Chapter 5*     Ode to a Flower                     143

**Into the Rose Garden**
*by Michael Pollan*                                145
**The Tulip**
*by Anna Pavord*                                   157
**Daylilies**
*by Sydney Eddison*                                181
**Cultivating Delight**
*by Diane Ackerman*                                195
**Orchid Fever**
*by Susan Orlean*                                  205

*Chapter 6*     On the Mend in the Garden           221

**A Garden Cultivates Pure Joy**
*by Dayle Allen Shockley*                          223
**In Grammy's Garden**
*by Lela Nargi*                                    231
**Ashes to Ashes**
*by Domenica Di Piazza*                            241
**Listening to My Garden**
*by Kathie Bailey*                                 249

Planning the Garden, by Charles Kinghan,
*The Farmer's Wife* magazine, March 1939

# INTRODUCTION

I took my first steps into gardening eleven years ago when my husband and I bought our first house in Minneapolis, Minnesota, with a yard that was, for the most part, a blank canvas. Aside from two small, raised gardens along the front and south side of the house and a couple of pathetic-looking tiger lilies pushing up through grass on the north side of the house, there was nothing.

When the gardening catalogs arrived the following spring, I placed an order with Spring Hill for an entire garden to fill the existing bed in front. As soon as the boxes arrived, packed with roots and bulbs for Asiatic lilies, daylilies, bleeding hearts, ferns, lilies of the valley, monardas, and forget-me-nots, I headed out to the front yard, armed with a spade and the Spring Hill garden map. The results of my labor that summer were unimpressive, but each spring the plants emerged from the earth more vigorous and lovely than the year before.

Encouraged by early success, my husband and I began to dig new gardens around the yard. We dug a border along the fence on the north side of the backyard and planted morning glories, daylilies, brown-eyed Susans, cone flowers, and fern-leaf bleeding hearts. We removed the narrow strip of grass that grew between the north side of the house and the neighbor's fence to create a shade garden, complete with stepping stones, Irish moss, ferns, tiger lilies, and English wood hyacinths.

On the sunny south side of the house we installed a raised vegetable bed and filled it with tomato plants, green pepper plants, carrots, lettuce, and green beans. Growing vegetables made me realize that each year in the garden is a learning experience, filled with trial and error. The next year I thinned the carrots vigorously, planted fewer tomato plants, and chose varieties that would bear fruit earlier in our too-short growing season.

Through the generosity of neighbors, friends, and family, I planted twenty-year-old peonies in a bank along the south side of the house. Ribbon grass and wild geraniums filled the space between the alley and garage. I scattered antique pink-and-gold irises from my father's yard around my own and added a cutting from a light-pink rose that had been in my husband's family for generations to a sheltered corner of the house. These plants had a story to tell, and it is this part of gardening that I enjoy most. I find it comforting to walk around the yard and be reminded of the friends and family who've shared what they've grown.

It would be these plants with a history, not the ones I had purchased myself through catalogs and gardening stores, that I would miss the most when we made the decision to move to a bigger house in

Gardening Together, vintage photograph, July 1941

the same neighborhood four years later. We were fortunate to have an unusually mild November in the days following the sale of the house, so we pirated a few plants we couldn't bear to leave behind—the irises, of course, because my dad had died the year before and they served as a pleasant reminder of him; the light-pink rosebush, which was a descendent of the plant that had supplied the flowers for my husband's grandmother's wedding bouquet; and a yellow rose that a friend had given me for my birthday that year.

The following spring we began tending a new garden in our new home. Although this time we had a few established gardens with which to work, we still had plenty to do to make the new garden our own. Five years later, after moving some plants and removing others, adding new plants only to take them out again a year later, digging new gardens and adding to the old ones, and installing a flagstone patio, we are getting closer to the garden we envision, but we're not there yet. Who knows if we'll ever feel as if the garden is really finished? To me, it is the process of creating and maintaining a garden that makes it all worthwhile. That tour I take at the end of each day to check on the progress of various plants is the real reward.

Pulling together the stories that appear in *The Gardener's Bedside Reader* was much like gathering the plants for a garden. In fact, some of the neighbors who had donated plants to my first garden also graciously offered me piles of gardening books from which to cull essays. And, in the generous spirit for which gardeners are well known, I met more than one writer along the way who would suggest another, who would suggest another.... Before I knew it, this collection of diverse stories from writers such as Jamaica Kincaid, Diane Ackerman, Susan Orlean, Wayne Winterrowd, Joe Eck, Lee May, Tovah Martin, Suzy Bales, Dan Hinkley, Ann Lovejoy, Michael Pollan, Vita Sackville-West, and Henry Mitchell had taken root, becoming the book you hold in your hands. Whether this collection sees you through the darkest winter days or accompanies you to that favorite garden bench during a well-deserved break from weeding and watering, my hope is that you find kinship and inspiration among these pages.

I shall never have the garden I have in my mind, but that for me is the joy of it; certain things can never be realized and so all the more reason to attempt them. A garden, no matter how good it is, must never completely satisfy. The world as we know it, after all, began in a very good garden, a completely satisfying garden—Paradise—but after a while the owner and the occupants wanted more.

—Jamaica Kincaid, *My Garden (Book)*, 1999

# Chapter 1

# The Perfect Garden

*Opposite:* **The Perfect Garden,** *Photograph © Richard W. Brown*

*Above:* Tuileries Garden, Paris blueprint, designed in 1664 by
Le Notre, the gardener of King Louis the Fourteenth

# Arcadia

*by Dan Hinkley*

When Dan Hinkley and his partner, Robert Jones, began the now world-famous Heronswood Nursery near Kingston, Washington, in 1985, they had no idea what it would blossom into. The five-acre garden is home to almost 10,000 species of plants that Hinkley meticulously tracked down around the globe. Hinkley not only found the plants, but for many years he wrote detailed and sometimes quirky descriptions of every plant that appeared in the Heronswood catalog. Hinkley would open each issue of the catalog with a personal essay. The following essay appeared in one of the first issues.

*Opposite:* Wisteria frames the water gardens at Giverny gardens in France, immortalized in the paintings of Claude Monet, *Photograph* © *Jerry Harpur*

How we wish to believe that an ideal exists, the garden of our minds, accurate and precise. It rains at night, just so softly, yet still it soaks the earth. Varmints live off weeds, which are rarely encountered. Slugs ooze beyond the hosta, which remains unblemished through the season. Fruits and vegetables are bountiful, while the continuum of perennials and flowering shrubs remains a never-ending crescendo from the first of spring until late autumn. No staking necessary.

This is not my garden. Yet I am left with the vestiges of an Arcadian desire, birthed by Brown's romantic landscapes and the dandyism of Montesquieu and Whistler, which makes me wish that somehow it was. In pursuing the consummate garden, I have discovered the conflicts that sabotage earthly perfection. Plants get aphids. Sometimes they die inexplicably. The desired continuum of seasonal interest is dashed by crashing waves of overgrown plants and retreating colors. In late summer, my real garden is crumpled like a little boy's dollar bill, held too tightly and too long.

Yet it is precisely the experience of imperfection that fuels my desire to continue. The plants are not staked, but certainly next year they will be. The combinations were good, but . . . The weeding was adequate, but . . . It allows us as gardeners the time to set aside any thoughts of Arcadia and capture if but briefly a moment of heavenly beauty; a germinating seed, unfolding leaves caught by early light, embracing fully the essence of a simple flower. It permits, in the words of Claes Oldenburg, slow study and respect for small things.

Comfort in this realization that it never will be perfect shall nonetheless not keep me from trying to make my garden better. The longer that I garden, the more I realize that it is only here that I will be nearest the unobtainable. As gardeners, we know in our hearts that there is no Arcadia. In that thought, I cannot help but feel the irony; that I was first exposed to gardening at the youngest age by my mother's father, who gardened on the northern shores of Lake Michigan, in a place they called Arcadia.

Roses and snapdragons in a cottage garden, *Photograph* © *Richard Felber*

LILIUM
RUBRUM

HELIANTHUS
HARDY SUNFLOWER

YUCCA
FILAMENTOSA
ADAMS
NEEDLE

PEONY
M. JULES ELIE

DELPHINIUM
PERENNIAL
LARKSPUR

RUDBECKIA
PURPUREA
PURPLE CONE
FLOWER

IRIS GERMANICA
DARIUS

# The Garden
# I Have in
# My Mind

*by Jamaica Kincaid*

An avid gardener and prolific writer, Jamaica Kincaid was born Elaine

Potter Richardson on the island of Antigua in 1949. Kincaid moved to

New York in 1965 and began to write for *Ingenue* magazine in the early

1970s. Before long she had landed a job with the *New Yorker*, where

she wrote the "Talk of the Town" column for many years. Kincaid has

written many novels, including *Annie John, Lucy,* and *Autobiography of My*

*Mother.* This piece was first published in her gardening memoir

*My Garden (Book).* It is printed here by permission of Farrar, Straus

and Giroux.

*Opposite:* Flowers for a perfect garden, *Burpee's Offering* catalog, 1917

I know gardeners well (or at least I think I do, for I am a gardener, too, but I experience gardening as an act of utter futility). I know their fickleness, I know their weakness for wanting in their own gardens the thing they have never seen before, or never possessed before, or saw in a garden (their friends'), something which they do not have and would like to have (though what they really like and envy—and especially that, envy—is the entire garden they are seeing, but as a disguise they focus on just one thing: the Mexican poppies, the giant butter burr, the extremely plump blooms of white, purple, black, pink, green, or the hellebores emerging from the cold, damp, and brown earth).

I would not be surprised if every gardener I asked had something definite that he or she liked or envied. Gardeners always have something they like intensely and in particular, right at the moment you engage them in the reality of the borders they cultivate, the space in the garden they occupy; at any moment, they like in particular this, or they like in particular that, nothing in front of them (that is, in the borders they cultivate, the space in the garden they occupy) is repulsive and fills them with hatred, or this thing would not be in front of them. They only love, and they only love in the moment; when the moment has passed, they love the memory of the moment, they love the memory of that particular plant or that particular bloom, but the plant of the bloom itself they have moved on from, they have left it behind for something else, something new, especially something from far away, and from so far away, a place where they will never live (occupy, cultivate; the Himalayas, just for an example).

Of all the benefits that come from having endured childhood (for it is something to which we must submit, no matter how beautiful we find it, no matter how enjoyable it has been), certainly among them will be the garden and the desire to be involved with gardening. A gardener's grandmother will have grown such and such a rose, and the smell of that rose at dusk (for flowers always seem to be most fragrant at the end of the day, as if that, smelling, was the last thing to do before going to sleep), when the gardener was a child and walking in the grandmother's footsteps as she went about her business in her garden—the memory of that smell of the rose combined with the memory of that smell of the grandmother's skirt will forever inform and influence the life of the gardener, inside or outside the garden itself. And so in a conversation with such a person (a gardener), a sentence, a thought that goes something like this—"You know, when I was such and such an age, I went to the market for a reason that is no longer of any particular interest to me, but it was there I saw for the first time something that I have never and can never forget"—floats out into the clear air, and the person from whom these words or this thought emanates is standing in front of you all bare and trembly, full of feeling, full of memory. Memory is a gardener's real palette; memory as it summons up the past, memory as it shapes the present, memory as it dictates the future.

I have never been able to grow *Meconopsis betonicifolia* with success (it sits there, a green rosette of leaves looking at me, with no bloom. I look back at it myself, without a pleasing countenance), but the picture of it that I have in my mind, a picture made up of memory (I saw it some time ago), a picture made up of "to come" (the future, which is the opposite of remembering), is so intense that whatever happens between me and this plant will never satisfy the picture I have of it (the past remembered, the past to come). I first saw it *(Meconopsis betonicifolia)* in Wayne Winterrowd's garden (a garden he shares with that other garden eminence Joe Eck), and I shall never see this plant (in flower or not, in the wild or cultivated) again without thinking of him (of them, really—he and Joe Eck) and saying to myself, It shall never look quite like this (the way I saw it in their garden), for in their garden it was itself and beyond comparison (whatever that amounts to right now, whatever that might ultimately turn out to be), and I will always want it to look that way, growing comfortably in the mountains of Vermont, so far away from the place to which it is endemic, so far away from the place in which it was natural, unnoticed, and so going about its own peculiar ways of perpetuating itself (perennial, biannual, monocarpic, or not).

I first came to the garden with practicality in mind, a real beginning that would lead to a real end: where to get this, how to grow that. Where to get this was always nearby, a nursery was never too far away;

HOME GARDENING No.541 VOL.21 JULY 16 1938 (Registered at the G.P.O. as a Newspaper)

# RAISING HERBACEOUS BORDER PLANTS FROM SEED

# HOME GARDENING

**2d.**

EVERY
FRIDAY

No.541
JULY 16 1938

## JOYOUS FLOWERS FOR YOUR SHADED BEDS

### YOU SOW FOXGLOVES NOW

how to grow that led me to acquire volume upon volume, books all with the same advice (likes shade, does not tolerate lime, needs staking), but in the end I came to know how to grow the things I like to grow through looking—at other people's gardens. I imagine they acquired knowledge of such things in much the same way—looking and looking at somebody else's garden.

But we who covet our neighbor's garden must finally return to our own, with all its ups and downs, its disappointments, its rewards. We come to it with a blindness, plus a jumble of feelings that mere language (as far as I can see) seems inadequate to express, to define an attachment that is so ordinary: a plant loved especially for something endemic to it (it cannot help its situation: it loves the wet, it loves the dry, it reminds the person seeing it of a wave or a waterfall or some event that contains so personal an experience as when my mother would not allow me to do something I particularly wanted to do and in my misery I noticed that the frangipani tree was in bloom).

I shall never have the garden I have in my mind, but that for me is the joy of it; certain things can never be realized and so all the more reason to attempt them. A garden, no matter how good it is, must never completely satisfy. The world as we know it, after all, began in a very good garden, a completely satisfying garden—Paradise—but after a while the owner and the occupants wanted more.

*Opposite: "Joyous Flowers for Your Shaded Beds," Home Gardening, July 16, 1938*

Formal Garden, *Photograph* © *Richard Felber*

# How Does Your Garden Grow? Any Way You Choose

*by Henry Mitchell*

*T*he following essay is one of many penned by Henry Mitchell between 1973 and 1993, when he wrote his popular "Earthman" gardening column. Mitchell was, without a doubt, one of the most entertaining gardening writers of our time. His columns have been collected into three books: *The Essential Earthman* (Indiana University Press, 1981), *One Man's Garden* (Houghton Mifflin, 1992), and *Henry Mitchell on Gardening* (Houghton Mifflin, 1998), in which this particular piece appeared.

Gardens are like people's lives: they aim at different goals, all more or less legitimate. But this means a superb garden of one type will draw only blank astonishment from a gardener whose plot is of another type.

Gertrude Jekyll, the eminent Edwardian gardener, designed her garden to "paint pictures" with living plants. She thought of it as a landscape in three dimensions, but with color and shapes used as a painter might use them.

André Lenôtre, the great French gardener of the seventeenth century, thought a garden should be a background for court ceremonial and should therefore have fabulously wide spaces for promenades and plenty of fountains as well as smooth reflecting pools.

E. A. Bowles, a great English gardener, thought the garden should be a collection of favorite plants, including oddities valued only for themselves and that did not count at all in the general picture.

Some gardens aim at neat, orderly surroundings to a house, in which the garden looks good throughout the year, preferably with little labor needed. Such a garden relies on masses of green, plenty of paving interesting textures, but with no attention given to flowering plants except as incidentals.

Others strive to reproduce a natural woodland or meadow, sometimes enriching a natural landscape with native or even exotic plants. Thus, a woodland may look wild and untouched, but with clumps of lilies not originally found in it, and perhaps drifts of daffodils and fall crocuses that would never be in that woodland unless planted by man.

Or a seemingly natural meadow could be made more flowery by introducing cornflowers, poppies, butterfly weed, buddleia, various California wildflowers, wild tulips from Asia Minor, and so forth. The meadow would still look wild but would have a great deal more color than an untouched meadow would ever have.

A water garden might consist of great rectangular pools set with masonry copings, or the water might be designed to look like a woodland pond overhung with willows. In each case there might be scarlet goldfish and water lilies of red, yellow, or blue, none of which would ever be found in a truly wild pond of that particular region.

A quite pretty garden could be an orchard, with the trees not too closely spaced, and beneath there might be a meadow garden packed with bright flowers from bulbs and other exotic—that is, nonnative—plants.

Popular now is the cottage garden, in which small trees, bulbs, roses, old-fashioned flowers (foxgloves, hollyhocks, larkspurs, valerian, and so on), and perhaps tomatoes, beans, and cabbages are all planted seemingly quite at random.

Quite apart from all these kinds of gardens based on different aesthetics and different ways of living, gardens even within one category will vary depending on the owner's wallet and his idea of what the garden means to him. A garden with a mainten-

Foxglove, lupine, parsley, and golden sage in Suzy Bales' garden, *Photograph © Suzy Bales*

ance budget of $150 a year may differ astonishingly from one on which $4,000 a year is spent, even though both gardens are the same type, even of the same design.

In my own garden I have no paid labor. I do it all myself. This is partly because I am tight with money, partly because I am not rich, but mostly because I don't like other people pawing over my treasures.

My approach would never do if the aim were to view the garden as a painted landscape or a composition of geometric forms. My garden will always be a cottage garden, though with some slight attention to mass effects (on a small scale). It will always give preference to plants over anything else. In back of all that is my personal view (no better or worse than dozens of other gardening views) that the place is so personal I cannot even hire anybody to weed or trim shrubs or sweep bricks or set tiles in the raised walls of a fish pool or build a shed or a summerhouse.

I well know I have neither the time nor the energy nor even the desire to have a garden that people admire. It is not for them but for me. I attach far more importance to the progress of the plants—the cycle of growth and decay—than to the floral display of the moment or to the effects of open space. If I want a few tiger lilies, as I certainly do, and if the best site for them happens to be beside a crimson shrub rose, then that's where they go.

My daylilies are almost all yellow or pastel melon colors, but if I happen to love a six-foot-tall wild daylily like *Hemerocaiis altissima*, I do not hesitate to include it, and the same goes for the night-blooming wild *H. citrina*, which looks sad all day long.

Whatever the underlying philosophy happens to be, almost every gardener will pay some attention to contrasts of texture and color and will give some thought to the aesthetic effect of paths and benches and sheds.

Gardens are not quite so different from one another as you might think at first. Even Versailles has some attractive plants in it, and even a jumble of marigolds, petunias, cleomes, chicory tomatoes, and onions presided over by a fig tree against a shack—even in such a garden there is often a degree of self-conscious attention paid to the aesthetics of the arrangement.

As long as there are plants at all, and as long as the gardener is human, and as long as the garden is an important part of the gardener's leisure, there will be a bond or a spirit between all gardens of whatever type.

Opposite: A formal garden at Barnsley House in Gloucester County, United Kingdom, designed by Rosemary Verey, *Photograph* © *Jerry Harpur*

HOME GARDENING   No.548   VOL. 21   SEPTEMBER 3 1938   *(Registered at the G.P.O. as a Newspaper)*

# RAISING HOME-GROWN ROSE TREES FOR YOUR GARDEN

# HOME GARDENING

EVERY FRIDAY

## 2ᵈ

No.548
SEPT. 3 1938

### HOW TO GROW WINTER VIOLETS
SEE SPECIAL ARTICLE

Winter violets, *Home Gardening* magazine, September 3, 1938

# Excerpt from
# In Your Garden,
# February 1948

*by Vita Sackville-West*

Between 1946 and 1961, novelist Vita Sackville-West wrote a weekly

gardening column for the London *Observer*. The columns were brief, but

packed with the insight and knowledge she obtained while creating the

famous gardens at Sissinghurst Castle in Kent. In the following piece,

which appeared in her book *In Your Garden*, published by Frances

Lincoln, Sackville-West dreams of filling a room with exotic plants

from around the world.

It is agreeable sometimes to turn for a change from the dutifully practical aspects of gardening to the consideration of something strange, whether we can hope to grow it for ourselves or not. A wet January evening seemed just the time for such an indulgence of dreams, and in an instant I found my room (which hitherto had boasted only a few modest bulbs in bowls) filling up with flowers of the queerest colours, shapes, and habits. The first batch to appear, thus miraculously conjured out of the air, were all of that peculiar blue-green which one observes in verdigris on an old copper, in a peacock's feather, on the back of a beetle, or in the sea where the shallows meet the deep.

First came a slender South African, *Ixia viridflora*, with green flowers shot with cobalt blue and a purple splotch: this I had once grown in a very gritty pan in a cold greenhouse, and was pleased to see again. Then came the tiny sea-green Persian iris, only three inches high, which I had seen piercing its native desert but had never persuaded into producing a single flower here. Then came *Delphinium macrocentrum*, an East African, which I had never seen at all, but which is said to rival the Chilean *Puya alpestris* in colouring.

*Puya alpestris* I knew. A ferocious-looking plant, and reluctant. Seven years had I cherished that thing in a pot, before it finally decided to flower. Then it threw up a spike and astonished everybody with its wicked-looking peacock trumpets and orange anthers, and side-shoots on which, apparently, humming-birds were supposed to perch and pollinate the flower.

And now here it was again, in my room, this time accompanied by the humming-birds which had been lamentably absent when I had flowered it after seven years. There were quite a lot of birds in my room by now, as well as flowers. For *Strelitzia reginae* had also arrived, escorted by the little African sun-birds which perch and powder their breast-feathers with its pollen. It is rare for plants to choose birds as pollinators instead of insects; and here were two of them. *Strelitzia reginae* itself looked like a bird, a wild, crested, pointed bird, floating on an orange boat under spiky sails of blue and orange. Although it had been

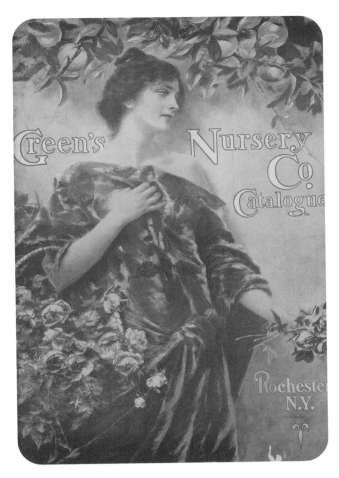

*Green's Nursery Co. Catalogue,* 1906

called regina after Queen Charlotte the consort of George III, I preferred it under its other name, the Bird of Paradise Flower.

Then, as a change to homeliness, came clumps of the old primroses I had tried so hard to grow in careful mixtures of leaf-mould and loam, but here they were, flourishing happily between the cracks of the floor-boards. Jack-in-the-Green, Prince Silverwings, Galligaskins, Tortoiseshell, Cloth of Gold; and as I saw them there in a wealth I had never been able to achieve, I remembered that the whole primula family

Poppies, phlox, and bachelor buttons, *Photograph © Suzy Bales*

was gregarious in its tastes and hated the loneliness of being one solitary, expensive little plant. They like huddling together, unlike the Lichens, which demand so little company that they will grow (in South America at any rate) strung out along the high isolation of telegraph wires.

There seemed indeed no end to the peculiarities of plants, whether they provided special perches for the convenience of their visitors, or turned carnivorous like the Pitcherplants. Why was it that the Vine grew from left to right in the Northern hemisphere, but refused to grow otherwise than from right to left in the Southern? Why was the poppy called *Macounii* found only on one tiny Arctic island in the Bering Sea and nowhere else in the world? How had it come there in the first place? In a room now overcrowded with blooms of the imagination *such* speculations flowed easily, to the exclusion of similar speculations on the equally curious behaviour of men.

The walls of the room melted away, giving place to a garden such as the Emperors of China once enjoyed, vast in extent, varied in landscape, a garden in which everything throve and the treasures of the earth were collected in beauty and brotherhood. But a log fell in the fire; a voice said: "This is the B.B.C. Home Service; here is the news," and I awoke.

# T

To dig in one's own earth,
with one's own spade,
does life hold anything better?

—Beverley Nichols, *Down the Garden Path*, 1932

*Chapter 2*

# The Nitty Gritty

*Opposite:* Hand trowel and lady's mantle, *Photograph © Jane Booth*

*Above:* Combined cultivator and seeder, *The True Temper Garden Book*, 1928

# Slug Boots:
## The Northwest's
## Answer to Pesticide

*by Ann Lovejoy*

Gardening is not for the faint of heart. When digging in the dirt, one is bound to encounter critters of all sorts, from the helpful worm to the harmful aphid and everything in between. In the following essay, renowned gardening author Ann Lovejoy provides a few tongue-in-cheek tips on how to combat the slimy slugs that plague gardens of the Northwest. Lovejoy, who lives and gardens on Washington's Bainbridge Island, has written more than a dozen books on gardening and is a regular contributor to a variety of gardening magazines. This piece originally appeared in her book *The Year in Bloom: Gardening for All Seasons in the Pacific Northwest*, published by Sasquatch Books in 1987.

Opposite: Betty Soloman tends to her lettuce patch, Alton, Rhode Island,
*Photograph © Jane Booth*

I recently read a delightful account of gardening in the Deep South in which the wise gardener never set foot into the garden patch without the protection of a sturdy pair of snake boots. Where snakes are plentiful, irritable and poisonous, it clearly pays to have half an inch of shoe leather between you and those curving fangs. Not only is your calf covered, you have a fairly deadly weapon of your own, right at foot. When deadly snakes rear their ugly little heads, you simply stomp them to belt material. Now, here in the Northwest, venomous snakes are not everyday fare, but another sinister and slimy character lurks beneath every leaf, waiting to attack the unsuspecting gardener. Anybody who has ever stepped barefoot on a large and squashy slug will immediately see both the charm and the application of this concept. Slug Boots. I like it.

Northwesterners would do well to emulate this custom, modified to the peculiar rigors and pests of our climate. To be really practical, slug boots must not be made of leather, which is unimproved by constant immersion in water, but of sleek, shining, supple, and sensuous plastic. The pair I finally settled on are fire engine red, with a determined little heel and a nicely patterned tread—not too deep, or it would defeat the whole purpose. Those slithery little buggers would curl up and hide in a deep tread. They are very sneaky, and very determined. Many people don't know just how serious a pest they can be. The day we found one exploring the depths of our Melitta coffeepot was the day I realized the extent of the problem. We all read the newspaper article about the electrical blackout up in Lakewood. A whole community lost its power thanks to the slime-trail of an errant slug making its leisurely way across a circuit board. We read it and chuckled; electricity, big deal. But nobody messes with my coffeepot. I got out those slug boots, tromped on that slug, and a few more I found lying around, and I was sold. You do need that tread, though, since the little suckers are slippery. I soon got

HAMMONDS SLUG-SHOT
1880   1915
USED SINCE 1880
AN INSECTICIDE FOR GARDEN USE

into the rhythm, something like clog dancing, and have been practicing assiduously ever since.

Now, we don't stoop to using much poison around here, since that would be politically and environmentally incorrect, but any of the widely available baits based on metaldehyde are acceptable, especially for those who simply can't dance. It attracts with the powerful allure of a blend of bran (which slugs find irresistible) and an alcohol analog that is fatally intoxicating. It is well known that slugs love to party; just leave a beer bottle in the garden overnight if you want proof. Set it on its side near the infant lettuce, with a tablespoon or so of beer left in it (any more would be a waste of B-vitamin complex). You are sure to find half a dozen crocked and reeling gastropods whooping it up in there in the morning. In my book, slugs are born to die anyway; surely this is an essentially thoughtful and gracious way to usher them out of this world?

If all this grisly death talk is too painful, you can simply speed slugs on their merry way, getting them out of your garden, but not necessarily all the way into slug heaven in one swoop. Just scoop one up, loosen up the old throwing arm and let fly. Slugs are great travelers, and any sensible one would quickly decide to skip the return trip to your yard, given such treatment. If you can't bear the idea of handling

*Above and opposite:* Vintage ads for slug killers, *Home Gardening* magazine

43

slugs, take advantage of a natural and symbiotic partnership; pick them up with a mollusk. It is not widely known that snails and slugs are mutually adhesive, but such is the case. Many souls who would sooner lose their lettuce than touch a slimy creature can toss a snail over the fence without much trouble. Next time you do this, look around for a baby slug, moosh it with the sticky part of your snail, and wish them bon voyage.

Since slugs are migratory, it isn't enough to empty the yard once a year. More will creep over the border at night, eluding the most vigilant patrols, to sup well at your salad bar before moving on. Snails have a less restless spirit. They are little homebodies; when they find a cozy place to sleep, in the crown of your favorite daylily, nestled among the agapanthus, or snuggled deep into the heart of a bulb, they develop a fondness for it and are very apt to return there day after day. You can take advantage of this habit by leaving a few bricks or boards around on the garden paths. Before too long, such spots become social centers, and you in your slug boots are the star turn.

There are a number of patented little fences and barriers which purport to be slug-proof, but nothing is really proof against the depredations of this slippery little character except the full weight of your disapproval. Actually, there are a few good tricks to try, other than the above-mentioned commercial bait, the most environmentally acceptable one around. Diatomaceous earth, generously sprinkled around the plants you want to keep, can keep those howling and snapping slugs at bay. It is particularly useful if pets or kids seem interested in the metaldehyde bait. (Both are fascinated by those little green plastic huts in which the bait is supposed to be protected from rain, which makes them more dangerous than useful.) The diatomaceous earth is made of the crushed exoskeletons of diatoms, tiny fossilized critters that are as brittle and sharp-edged as glass when pulverized. Harmless to humans and pets, the stuff punctures slugs and snails with hundreds of pinpricks as they crawl through it. That causes them to leak out all their innards, which is fairly final. It is, however, expensive.

An acquaintance of the family has earned his doctorate studying the ecology of banana slugs, and he has shown us a series of pictures which are really quite endearing. In them, a saucer of milk is set down, and one by one, the slugs approach, bending their little horns curiously, tasting the milk, at first cautiously, then avidly dipping in to the dish. The final shot of a whole tiny herd of slugs slurping is absolutely cute. A gardening friend recounts a fascinating tale of the courtship and mating ritual of slugs, as she observed it one fine day. Apparently, as slugs merge, a clear and crystalline droplet forms, dangling on a long thread and spreading slowly into a scalloped, pulsating sac. As the embrace is completed, the bag of living water is drawn up and reabsorbed. The process is lengthy, and as our friend

Tools of the Trade, Bill Whitney's Garden,
*Photograph © Jane Booth*

describes it, lovely and moving, almost lyrical. Perhaps we ought to reconsider, make room in our hearts for these little creatures, defenseless and guileless.

Well, maybe. But when I see another crop of promising seedlings mown down wholesale, a brand-new and long-awaited plant gnawed to the bare and quivering roots, the glossy new leaves of my miniature hostas tattered and ragged, I give no quarter. Let them eat metaldehyde! After all, it's not as if slugs are an endangered species. I do make a few concessions; I don't bait routinely, just when seedlings are rowed out, when seeds are sown, or when fragile treasures are transplanted. However, when I uncover a nest of gastropod eggs, round and shimmering like tiny pearls, those future sluglets and snailings go straight under the fierce little heels of my slug boots.

45

Hedda Kopf of Woodbridge, Connecticut, tends to her herb garden,
partially designed by Frederick and Mary Ann McGourty of Hillside Gardens,
*Photograph* © *Jane Booth*

# The Delights of
## Weeding *by Suzy Bales*

*We Grew It, A Book Dedicted
to the Fun of Gardening,* 1937

Award-winning garden writer Suzy Bales expounds on the sheer joy of

getting down on her hands and knees to pull those pesky weeds in the

following essay, which appeared in her book *Suzy Bales' Down-to-Earth*

*Gardener,* published by Rodale in 2004. Bales is also the author of *Gifts*

*from Your Garden, A Garden of Fragrance* (Harper Collins, 2000), and *The*

*Garden In Winter* (Rodale, 2007). Her work has also been featured in

*Better Homes and Gardens, Horticulture,* and the *New York Times.*

Speaking as a gardener, I don't think you can get more down-to-earth than weeding. My weeding has never been planned and I don't wake up and say, "Today I'll weed the kitchen garden." Nor do I choose a day in advance on a calendar. Weeding is usually spontaneous. I start off walking through the garden to see what's in bloom, to check which seeds have germinated, to water, and so on. Before I know it, I'm sidetracked into weeding. Dealing with weeds is like eating potato chips: You can never pull just one. Sometimes an hour passes before I'm vertical once more and back on the path I started out on.

When walking through the garden with friends, I may absent-mindedly pluck a weed or two and toss them under the nearest shrub to decompose. Nongardeners find this quite shocking, but that's nature's way. After a major cleanup, most weeds end up in the compost pile. If they are about to go to seed, I dump them in the trash.

Friends who don't garden can't accept the idea that I am enjoying myself when I'm weeding. The myth that it's drudgery, an unpleasant chore, is too much with us. Truth be told, weeding is a stolen pleasure, time all to myself. The monotonous rhythm of repeated action allows

A garden in transition, *Photograph © Jane Booth*

my mind to wander—my imagination unclogs, and the frustrations of daily life are washed away with the glow of perspiration.

My pleasure in weeding increases after a soaking rain, when even onion grass, dock, bindweed, lamb's-quarters, shepherd's purse, and chrysanthemum weed, all my most tenacious weeds, can be pulled out whole from the soft ground without a trowel. If it's warm enough, I like to weed in a gentle rain.

As my mind drifts, my eye records what is happening in the garden. Often I end up sitting or sprawling at the edge of a border to avoid stepping into the bed and compressing the soil. Reaching in and under the plants, I've found myself in positions that might tax a circus contortionist. But by bending down, kneeling, squatting, or even lying on the ground, you can get such an intimate view of the world of plants.

There is much to be learned, but not all of it is pleasant. A streak of silvery slime on the ground or over a leaf tells me slugs have taken up residence. Squelching slugs is a great sport, but not for the squeamish. If I weren't at ground level, I might not have noticed what was afoot until huge chunks were missing from the leaves. Or I might spot a scurry of sow bugs, one of the garden's beneficial decomposers, usually a sign of a decaying plant nearby. What lurks in the shadows is often the clue to solving a plant mystery or catching a destructive culprit before the damage is done.

More often, however, this close-in approach opens windows into the wonders of the garden. Peering at the innocent, brightly colored, intricately designed, and seemingly expectant faces of violets and their many relatives, I am in awe of the handiwork of Mother Nature. She never seems to repeat herself.

I grew native North American violets for decades before I noticed last September tiny nodding purple buds under their heart-shaped leaves, an inch or two above the ground. I kept an eye on them all fall, thinking that perhaps they had been nudged by summer drought to bloom out of season, but they never did. Trying to find an answer, I consulted the perennials expert, Dr. Allan Armitage. He explained that true violets produce two different kinds of flowers. The showy spring flowers I love to pick are infertile. Consequently, later in the season, another set of flowers that never open form at the base of the plant. They are known as *cleistogamous* flowers, and their sole purpose is to self-pollinate within the closed bud and to form seeds. These flowers have the ability to spew their small seeds up to 9 feet from the plant. Checking back under the leaves later in fall, I found the dried, open seed capsules.

## If You Don't Know It, Don't Pull It

Weeding can be a treasure hunt as well as a simple cleanup. Learning to identify seedlings is a necessity if we hope to accept nature's gifts. In any case, exercise care. If I don't know it, I don't pull it. It's a gamble to let it grow, yet I often get lucky. (It's my idea of living dangerously.) Of course, I first check to see if the mystery seedling is part of a group found in only one part of the garden. If it is, the probability is high that the mother plant is nearby. If it's a lonely specimen, it could have been dropped by a bird, carried in with the mulch, floated in on a breeze and parachuted down, or unknowingly smuggled in on the back of our dog. But if it's a weed, chances are that others like it will be scattered widely. Still, appearances can be deceiving: Remember that the first leaves on a brand-new plant are cotyledons, not true leaves, so wait until the true leaves are evident before making a positive identification.

In a garden, new seedlings appear daily. Some are showy: The red leaves of amaranth give it away. Some are gawky: A tulip tree seedling has tulip-shaped leaves too big for its britches. Some are ferny: Nigella, a miniature of its mother, is all aflutter in a light breeze. And some are instantly identifiable: Lupine, for example, has its foliage arranged in tight whorls. Once I'd learned to recognize my favorites, I let them be or scoop them up and move them to a better spot. Extras are always welcome gifts to neighbors and friends.

Morning glories would, if they could, take over the earth. Besides their glorious good looks, I grow them so curious children can pinch their puffed buds and hear them pop. Each flower blooms for only a day before it literally goes to seed. "Heavenly Blue," a hybrid, drops hundreds of seeds over the course of its three- to four-month bloom by my estimation. Even if I wanted to, I couldn't wipe out the entire population with one swipe because the seeds don't germinate all at one time; they keep coming all summer and fall.

### Flowers of Discontent

Heading my list of unwelcome plants are the "flowers of discontent" that wander at will and stomp on everything in their way. We thoughtlessly introduced many of these, not taking the time to check their credentials. Spirea, for example, has taken over the path and driveway garden. The musk mallow (*Malva moschata*) has skipped to and fro across the length of the formal border. Gooseneck loosestrife's cocked head is scanning the woods, planning its advance. Clumps of purple loosestrife, the roadside menace, have suddenly appeared—two in the perennial garden, one in the meadow, and another at the top of the bank. This means all-out war.

"Glory of the Autumn Greenhouse: The Guernsey Lily," *Home Gardening*, June 25, 1938

Nursery salespeople and catalogs can be deafeningly silent about a plant's true habit. To be fair, a plant's behavior may depend greatly on where it is planted. Lady's mantle has been known for her promiscuity in other gardens, but in mine she is a lady—too much so, unfortunately. Her chartreuse locks are one of my favorites for poking into bouquets of roses. And I love the way she cradles raindrops in her leaves, where they delicately glisten like pearls in the sun.

Unfortunately, I've come to love many invasive perennials. I want to keep a few of each around, and that's the rub. With some of them, it's all or nothing. I know I have to pull up the excess spirea, musk mallow, and gooseneck loosestrife in spring. Others simply need to be placed in a correctional facility. Mint minds its manners if confined to a pot. Chives, too, must be imprisoned for life. The real troublemakers—purple loosestrife and creeping liriope come to mind—have to be yanked out by their feet and tossed in the garbage if we are to have anything else in the garden.

## Underground Discoveries

Weeding takes me underground, into the secret lives of plants. How else would I know about colorful roots? It is not something that you normally find in books. Ask most anyone, and they will likely say, "Roots are brown, silly."

When in bloom, gooseneck loosestrife is a quiet beauty with a gracefully arching head covered in alter-boy white starry flowers. Such looks are deceiving. Its true color shows underground, where you find scarlet roots that are the devil to dislodge. They run in all directions, sometimes several feet, before rearing into an angelic-looking plant. If the soil is moist and loamy, I can apply a slow, gentle pressure and pull out a foot or two at a time. If the soil is dry and crusted, Lord help me. I bring out the spading fork, employ brute strength, and begin the lifting. The only line of defense is hard work—or a cement barrier. I must warn you against dividing gooseneck strife regularly to keep it in check, as many garden writers recommend. Dividing it only helps it multiply. Luckily, the red runners are easy to spot when they come up

Suzy Bales' kitchen garden, *Photograph* © *Suzy Bales*

for air in spring. The red at the base of a small plant's stem is the signal for gardeners to take warning.

The bright white roots of creeping liriope *(Liriope spicata)* defy conventional wisdom. I made a big mistake by planting creeping liriope one time. Every family has its saints and sinners, and this one is a sinner. Conversely, cultivars of *L. muscan* are so well behaved you can take them anywhere. They slowly increase without an inclination to conquer. They are also better-looking, with wider leaves and showier flowers. I unfortunately let the creepy liriope, as I call it, roam far too long and cover too much ground. I will be removing it for years to come. Thankfully, the bright white runners are easy to spot—how do they stay so white romping in all that dirt?—but they are so plentiful that it's easy to miss a few. This is why, when weeding out a menace such as this one, I always revisit the area weekly to yank up new shoots.

If you see any of these pesky perennials growing in a friend's garden, I suggest that you dart in and pull them out without wasting a minute.

Dan Hinkley's Heronswood Gardens, *Photograph* © *Jerry Harpur*

# Growing
# Regret

*by Dan Hinkley*

All gardeners have a few regrets about what they haven't gotten around

to planting or about a plant they did indeed put in the ground, only to

watch it choke out other, often more desirable, garden plants. In his

essay "Growing Regret," Dan Hinkley of Heronswood Nursery in

Washington State runs through his list of gardening-related regrets.

Regular visitors to the Heronswood website might recognize this piece,

as it was posted on the site for a time.

As I have this year regretfully and unilaterally invaded my fifth decade of living, I have noticed here and there the abrupt appearance of bodily bulges. Upon inspection, I find these to be pocketfuls of gathered regrets, those disappointing things accumulated over the years rooted in some deed done or left undone, at last manifesting in my ripening age. My life thus far, not remorsefully in the least, has been fed and nurtured by a garden in one form or another. And though I too have sizeable swellings of social and personal shoulda couldas, the bulk of these regrets have been gleaned from the dirt or the garden above.

I possess a voluminous regret for believing in color. Young gardeners are impressionable and pure and believe that one must be faithful to the cause and bow to the prophets, who subscribe to color, to rise respectfully within this craft of gardening. Once elevated, they too can cattily criticize the colors in other gardens, most of which are young. It was a waste of my time. Colorist gardens for the sake of effect without good horticulture, as many are, are simple and shallow. It is using pigment rather than plants, adjective rather than noun, forcing drama rather than creating dialogue between plant and space.

I once considered combining a living animal with a plant in my garden. It was an epiphany. Our sweet fat cat had beautiful black hair with a marbling of tawny brown throughout her coat. She looked simply swell when resting amongst our patch of black lily turf in our back yard, the ebony colored foliage of this plant resounding as a superb background to felinaceous fur. The manure mulch was reflected handsomely in her coat's interlacings of chocolate. I deliberated ways to keep this sweet animal in exactly that place during social events. I am sorry for the thoughts, thoughts that are mixed with the awareness that I really never was very talented in my attempts to create a colorist garden and the regrets of my inability to concede this shortcoming with grace.

I regret that I did not learn the contentment of making other gardeners feel bad about themselves earlier in my career. Through this, one becomes a better gardener and, thusly, a better person. For instance, Meconopsis, the Blue Himalayan Poppy, the holy grail. Gardeners in the Pacific Northwest are amongst the chosen few in North America that can bring these jealously blue poppies to fruition in our gardens. That fact alone is a prompt to plant more than we ever should.

I have many horticulturally induced friends from the Deep South and Southeast and Southwest who cannot possibly grow Meconopsis. When they visit us in early summer, just when the flocks of Meconopsis are at their finest, I wait until the western light has winged below the limbs of Douglas Firs in our woodland. Then, with glasses of wine in hand—a reasonable and fruity Chablis—I suggest a saunter through the garden, with the endpoint, known only to me, being my motherlode of blue envy. In this form of botanical S&Meconopsis, it is important that you personally do not notice your cerulean drifts before your, ahh, participants. When they do at last, you must then stoop down and extract a handful of Meconopsis seedlings from the bed, discard them on the path and step on them, while declaring in as serious a tone as you can muster, "These Meconopsis are SO weedy." It makes you feel warm inside.

We all want something thriving in our gardens that should not be there. While indeed it is a boring thing to choose too conservatively the palette of plants you wish to cultivate, and push the envelope in regard to diversity, it is quite easy to be tempted to choose plants well outside of zonal realities. There are certain plants that simply do not like the perpetual coolness of our climate. They are the plants that march in place while all others sally forth. They diminish in size while others inflate. They are at first ugly and then they die. I wish I might have become more sensitive to the plight of these plants so abused in my garden, but it probably would not have made much difference. One benign winter and you watch adventurous spirits sprout like cress. Two consecutive mild winters, new chapters of the Hardy Citrus Society begin to appear in the Greater Puget Sound; after the third, just prior to a full-bore Arctic outbreak, our landscapes have morphed into a Bacardi Dark ad. I have been sorrowfully and repeatedly sucked into the zonal bending vortex of our mostly mild-mannered but regularly bitchy climate. After the freeze thaws, the garden melts and I feel a rather large lump forming directly behind my wallet.

In my raincoat pocket are swelling the apologies for believing that I might have gracefully pruned my exquisite specimen of Japanese Maple, coaxing forth its superb, inherent silhouette, all the while listening to the Mariners play at Yankee Stadium on my headset.

A gardener at Campo de' Fiori, *Photograph* © *Jane Booth*

"Here we go! Ichiro on third, Boonie on second, top of the ninth, nobody out, and here comes Edgar!"

I lift my pruning saw in a Zenlike trance. I am surgeon. I am artist. I am Ichiro.

"My oh my, this is a whole new ballgame, and maybe a whole new series!"

I stretch my saw straight out to the tree while adjusting the sleeve of my raincoat at the right shoulder.

"Here comes the first pitch from Rivera and Edgar belts it hard up the middle."

I begin sawing really fast, lost in the zone.

"Jeter leaps high to his left and makes an UNBELIEVABLE catch, he fires the ball toward Posada at home, he's GOT Ichiro, Boonie towards third, Posada struggles to stand and fires to Aaron Boone, Boonie dives in head first. He got him, he got him, Boonie's out by Aaron Boone. Holy Cow. UNBELIEVABLE, THE MARINERS HAVE BEEN TRIPLED OUT. THE GAME IS OVER!"

My Mariners. My tree. My oh my.

I believe in getting even. And more so, my regrets for not doing so more often is found stashed in innumerable pockets. My gardening friends in Vermont, for example, insisted that I take a division of *Mentha buddleifolium* "Variegatum" when I visited them three years ago. "It is very good value," I was told in a pretentious and potty voice. It was also a very generous division, a transaction that should have been flagged as suspicious from the start. It grew well in my garden the first year. The second, we clocked it weaving the borders at five miles/hour. Over the course of a month, as I meticulously chivvied and unearthed each warp and woof of root, I mentally wrote the note attending the care package

I would send my friends. "Dear Boys," I would ultimately write, "we have come to simply adore the frilly texture and undaunted courage of the plant I am sending along. It is of particularly good caliber." Lamentably, I derive exceptional pleasure in picturing their garden awash in the filigreed emerald green of horsetail.

I am remorseful that for as many years as I have been making gardens, I remain incapable of spacing my prepubescent plants in the garden with their ultimate size at maturity in mind. These are big regrets and add many notches to the belt. It is not as if I don't participate in a conversation with myself as I am placing the pots before digging the holes. We generally have a pretty good row with one another. I lose. Four-inch pots of infantile perennials or shrubs look unconditionally ludicrous spaced six feet apart. Impatience and the desire to possess a prideful thing after a week's work prevails. In late April, a warm rain soaks the ground and within minutes plants swell faster than a dieter being let off the Atkins bus in front of a Cinnabun

*True Temper Garden Book, 1928*

Factory Outlet. The borders are annexed by steroidal specimens assuming the graces of a 1960s East German Olympic women's track team. It is an opprobrious action fundamental to the most shameful of my regrets: impatience.

I have never raised children other than several endearing dogs that, in my mind, resemble tolerably well-behaved children with cold noses. I could not imagine wishing away the puppy-ness of my dogs, so I can only assume that most parents feel quite the same about their brood except perhaps during their second year. So why is that we wish away the youngness of our gardens? In a wink, the seedlings we coddle are already trees and the small divisions of perennials fill the void and puerile vines mature and secure the arbor. There is no revisiting the childlike garden short of moving and starting it once again, itself unthinkable as we too are no longer youthful but bloated with years and many regrets.

Yet it is exactly this that I will do, once again, as I strive to make another garden and make it the most beautiful garden in the world. I will again scribble my passion upon a canvas of open ground, and stand with a presidentially dazed expression on my face, a gallon pot under my arm, revolving like the human lighthouse, looking for the very best place to tuck it in the ground. As I do, I will reflect on those nascent days of my first garden and the bosom of guilt that would blossom in me for having done just that, retreating indoors at dark, mentally exhausted and feeling as if I had accomplished nothing at all. In retrospect, those were my most productive moments. My garden was in fact planted through the moments that I had believed to have been lost.

So I will not regret these moments again ever, as I attempt, in my mind, to psychically create the most precise of color combinations, with plants too tender, too aggressive, planted too close together from friends too generous while listening to the Mariners play on my headset. And with each pot that I place in the earth, I will extract a few regrets from my pockets stuffed here and there and gently plant them for future harvest.

# Good Luck Sure to Grow Seeds

## 1946

**SURPRISE FLOWER GARDEN**
GENEROUS PACKET FREE
WITH EVERY SEED ORDER

**GOOD LUCK SURE TO GROW**

# GOOD LUCK GARDENS
## PARADISE, PA.

ALL SEEDS AND MERCHANDISE SENT POSTPAID

# The Vine, or, Garden and Know Thyself

*by Sigrid Arnott*

Morning Glory, *Photograph* © *Suzy Bales*

*I*n the following essay, Sigrid Arnott, a gardener who lives and writes in Minneapolis, tackles the not-so-uncommon problem of hiding the unsightly yard of a neighbor by planting The Vine along her fence line.

*Opposite: Good Luck Gardens catalog, 1946*

It sometimes seems that my garden is maliciously bent on revealing my shameful secrets to the world. The embarrassment of airing one's dirty laundry is nothing compared to that of exposing the state of my backyard. My front yard may signal conformity with its bluegrass lawn and evergreen foundation plantings; containers filled with begonias and impatiens march up our front steps, suggesting that an organized plant waterer lives within. But, should you go around the side and enter the backyard, my garden will tell you the truth: "Lazy," say the weeds. "Profligate," whisper the rare and expensive (and dying) perennials. "Doesn't respect authority," chants the boisterous rosebush.

My garden has also helped me know my climate and myself. As a gardening neophyte, I was seduced by photos of gorgeous landscapes that I would try to re-create by purchasing and planting enchanting plants at assigned places within staked-out lines. Often those plants—placed where I thought their flowers would look good—smiled back at me for a few months and then politely faded away, leaving a convenient hole to plug with a new purchase.

I still find myself admiring certain garden styles, fantasizing over photos of tropical hideaways, or coveting flowery English cottage scenes. Yet, I know that to mine own soil, light, zone, and energy level I must be true. I have found the strength to bypass the flowers that need daily deadheading; the experience to resist the siren songs of tender tropicals; the courage to face my heavy clay soil with bushels of peat, sand, and compost; and the wisdom to know that I am too lazy to prune an espaliered fruit tree.

Now I consider the plant's needs before my own; I appreciate leaves as much as flowers; I don't care too much about a rose's accomplishments as long as it is healthy. I don't plant delicate plants near the dog's paths or expect an astilbe to bloom in drought. Yes, I have learned the limitations and possibilities of my little city plot, home to a family of four and a fetch-mad dog.

But recognizing these physical limitations isn't enough. The harder part has been learning what kind of a gardener I am, and this I have been taught by my yard. Like a mirror in which I hope to see my ideal, my garden reflects back a brutally honest image of reality. "Yes, I know delphiniums are nostalgic of your childhood," my yard repeats, "but you're an adult now and you have to find your own way to have tall, blue flowers." Or, "A Japanese garden could give you a feeling of tranquility, but do you feel calm looking at river stones in need of realignment?" Or, "I know you want to plant a new bed, but aren't you just

procrastinating weeding what you have already planted?" I have learned that I like big projects like changing the grade and installing a rain garden, as well as the mindless puttering of pinching back, staking up, and trimming, yet I hate regimented upkeep like lawn mowing or turning the compost pile.

Finally, after fifteen years in this spot, my garden and I seem to be at peace with our constraints and one another. The plants of Minnesota's woodlands (cimifuga, ferns, columbines, phlox, geraniums, etc.) coexist with the little-old-lady die-hards handed down from neighbors and family (iris, ferns, columbines, phlox, geraniums, etc.) in a vaguely Japanese-inspired yard.

Rockford Giant Phlox,
*Great Northern Seed Co.* catalog, 1905

Yet, gardening and knowing thyself is never static—you can't figure it out for once and always. In my case it has been The Vine that reminds of this truth. Pausing to consider it climbing along my fence, you might simply think "out-of-bounds and messy." But the vine laughs at me and says, "You can plant a vine view, but you can't hide!"

Although my yard has a tendency to get a little out-of-bounds, I try to keep the upper hand. Long before she had moved, my former neighbor, however, had given up.

After a few years of minimal maintenance, only a few stalwart perennials remained under the tangle of overgrown grasses and weeds that had flourished during her reign of neglect. On occasion (usually a lovely, breezy day when I was enjoying my yard with my children), she would emerge from her house to "garden." She might attempt to cut a few feet of grass before abandoning the strangled, overheated mower in a cloud of two-stroke gases. Or she would indiscriminately spray some herbicides on her lot, hack at some ragweed, and then return, defeated, back to her abode. At other times she was like a timid burrow dweller: she would open the back door a few inches, sense hostility in the thistles and brambles, and immediately retreat to the safety of her home. About once a year she would hire an unsuspecting youth trying to make a few dollars doing odd jobs, to cut her grass. Poor things, they never returned to the yard of horrors.

Worst of all, the former flower beds along the wire cyclone fence separating our yards sprouted Siberian elms that grew about 3 feet a month in Minnesota rain and sun. Although I could try and ignore her yard, I couldn't ignore this wall of weedy wood that choked out her bushes, then began strangling my nearby plants.

Vintage seed packets, Page's Seeds and Tregunno Seeds Limited

Can you tell she drove me crazy? That her gardening behavior (rather lack of it) became my obsession? Instead of gazing enraptured at the blooms spilling off my climbing rose, I watched in horror as broad-leaf herbicides drifted on *my* broad-leafed perennials and on the quilt I had spread for my son to play on. Instead of considering the lily (my lily), I agonized over her deadly nightshade vines creeping toward me. However much I tried to enjoy the flickering shadows cast by my lilacs, my head would snap in the direction of our lot line where the weedy Siberian elms blotted out my sunlight and sucked up my rainfall. It was torture.

If I could have just put up a tall board fence, I might have been OK. Unfortunately, I am morally opposed to tall, solid-wood fences. So I turned to my garden design books, and was advised to create a visual screen. The idea is that you plant a vine to climb up in front of an offensive view, thus obliterating it from your perspective. Interestingly, the visual distraction to be blotted out is usually the neighbors'. Because we can't actually plant a rambling rose on their Rambler (on blocks), we are advised to plant it in our little Eden between us and their wasteland.

Yes, I needed a vine to grow on the admittedly ugly chain-link fence dividing our yards, but which vine? There seemed to be many described as "suitable for screening," but the spot was a difficult one. Her trash trees left that side of the yard in full shade, and the root competition was fierce. A woman at the plant store said that maybe I needed a native plant; something tough that could survive under adverse conditions. So I chose the innocent-sounding river grape, which would also have some wildlife value. I imagined how the area would be transformed into a little arbor where cardinals would nibble miniature clusters of grapes while perching on cute, curling tendrils.

I knew not to expect much the first year. I had to hack and saw a hole through elm roots to plant the tiny vine. I hopefully reminded myself of the old saying, "First year sleep, second year creep, third year leap." As I gritted my teeth, leaned far across the fence, and surreptitiously pruned her branches coming in my direction, I was imagining the vine's roots extending down into the earth.

waste energy making strong, self-supporting trunks and branches, they can grow upward—fast.

Now there was no longer a bad view needing screening, yet the vine shifted into high gear. No longer content to cover the fence, it grabbed trees and grew up them at an indecent rate. Showing no respect for boundaries, it raced down to the alley, found the neighbors' back fence and covered it. It flopped off the fence and shamelessly went in search of anything vertical to grow on. It was an embarrassment. Whereas I used to lean far over the fence dividing our yards to cut my neighbor's tree branches, I now had to do the same thing as I tried to rein in and hack back my vine.

Of course, cutting back one's own plant is a pleasure compared with having to remove your neighbor's. The psychological energy I used to waste agonizing over my former neighbor's weeds was now channeled into new gardening projects. I planted a native woodland garden and experimented with new (and well-behaved!) clematis vines.

My new, industrious neighbors were busy, too. The first year in their house, they restored their lawn, trimmed trees, cut back my vine, and planted. Last year they began a large landscaping project. Old sidewalk was broken up and hauled out, and new pavers were delivered. (The Vine promptly covered all the materials they stored in the alley.) Then topsoil was removed in staked-out areas of a new sidewalk and patio, and subsurface crushed gravel was laid in and tamped down.

Because I needed soil to bank up around my foundation, I asked if I could take some dirt off their hands, and I was given permission to come over and help myself. I left my plot of flowers and delicate ferns and took my wheelbarrow next door, where I turned back to admire my property from their perspective. The house looked OK, but my pretty yard was screened by a monstrous vine. It waved at me and said, "You aren't fooling anyone with your wimpy maidenhair ferns! You know yourself: messy, random, not even self-supporting!"

The next day my back was sore from hauling all that dirt, but I didn't rest. I had a vine to trim. I pruned hard, chopped the trimmings into small pieces, and dumped them into the compost bin.

As I was chopping, more new materials were unloaded in my neighbors' driveway near my (vine-screened) compost bin.

"Another project?" I asked as they signed for the delivery.

"We decided to build a pergola over our patio. It will give a little shade, and maybe we'll even plant some vines to climb on it."

Lucky them; they won't have to plant vines to screen the view of the neighbors. The Vine can feel those vertical supports from my yard: it's on its way.

Nohora Yuille's stash of terra cotta pots, *Photograph © Jane Booth*

*Pivoine de la Chine.*

*Pæonia*

P. J. Redouté. _ 101.

Vic

# Among Heirloom Plants, Always Tread Lightly

*by Laura Billings*

The perfect bloom, Diana Felber's garden in
Housatonic, Mass., *Photograph © Jane Booth*

Laura Billings, columnist for *Mpls/St. Paul Magazine*, offers a cautionary

tale about making a new yard your own in her essay "Among Heirloom

Plants, Always Tread Lightly."

*Opposite: Pivoine de la Chine, P.J. Redouté_101*

73

It is a fact of home ownership that putting down roots will often require digging up someone else's. How you go about this can sow the seeds of a fruitful relationship with the neighbors, or sour it for the length of your adjusted-rate mortgage.

I'll start with a cautionary tale.

A few years ago, some friends of mine bought a charming but neglected little bungalow from a white-haired woman who had lived there for almost fifty years. The transaction was started on the sidewalk one night, and was completed over several pots of tea. The husband, a structural engineer by trade, outlined his plans to repair the rotting foundation of the garage. The wife, a designer by instinct, explained her plans to strip the layers of paint from the woodwork and reveal all the warm oak that lay underneath. The owner was so charmed by their enthusiasm for the hard work ahead, she happily accepted their offer and stopped by with a nice pound cake the day they moved in.

Rhododendron, *The Illustrated Dictionary of Gardening*,
circa 1900

Neighbors who walked by at night with their dogs nodded approvingly at the couple's obvious industry and the positive effect it would have on their property values. With the wood stripped and the garage saved, the couple turned their attention to a front porch rotted through by the roots of a huge, overgrown rhododendron.

The rhododendron was the jewel of the neighborhood, a great flowering mass of dark, waxy leaves and tissue-paper blooms. It was thought to be more than a hundred years old, and was of such an unusual and gorgeous variety that in the 1950s a local gardening league had used one of its branches to begin a botanical garden dedicated to all varieties of the plant. This particular rhodie was so hardy, and it blossomed so early in the spring and stayed full so long into summer that it had often served as a backdrop for photos of first communions and high school graduations; twice it had appeared as one of those seasonal illustrations on the front page of the local paper. Had it been a house instead of a plant, it might have qualified for historic preservation.

My friends did not learn this, however, until after a landscaping crew with a backhoe unclenched it from the earth and carted it away, drawn and quartered, on the back of a flatbed truck. That was when the neighbors, the ones who had been so welcoming just months before, turned on them.

"You know that rhodie you ripped out was probably the oldest one in the neighborhood, maybe even the county—"one of the neighbors would start to say.

"It had seen better days . . .," one of my friends would answer.

"And it was a really rare breed—" the neighbor would continue.

"But it was growing through the floor boards."

"That tree was that woman's pride and joy."

"We're sorry . . . we didn't know. . . ."

Once all the remodeling was complete, the couple held an open house to show friends and family—and particularly the neighbors— that it had all been worth it. But as the wife approached the new porch to bring lemonade to her guests, she heard them still discussing the day the rhododendron had been rooted out. While they had the good manners to compliment the couple's fine work when she reached the room, she understood then that no improvement would ever make up for the ruined rhododendron.

A few months later, she and her husband put the house on the market and moved a few blocks away. The only thing the new owners had to do to make their mark—and secure the love of their neighbors—was to plant a small rhododendron a few feet from where the larger one had been.

This story came back to me—and haunted me—the first time we came to tour the house that is now our home. Spreading its branches wide over our roof and three others was a truly majestic oak, with a trunk almost 10 feet around. Such a tree is a kind of public trust, I realized, just like the rhododendron. This was confirmed when, on our moving day, the neighbors showed up to discuss it.

"I would look into the tree," said the neighbor whose garage rests under its branches. "It might have wilt."

"But there are ways to deal with that," said the neighbor to her north.

"Besides cutting it down," continued the couple who live on the other side of the alley.

I understood their meaning at once and hired an arborist the next week. The diagnosis wasn't wilt, and I reassured each new neighbor I met that there would be no need to operate, congratulating myself on having survived the sort of landscaping landmine that had forced my friends to move.

Then summer came, and so did the peonies. According to local lore, they were first planted in the 1930s by one of the former owners, a woman who had divided them every few years, until they took over one side of the driveway, then the other, and then everywhere else with an empty patch of earth. Their names—Mrs. Franklin D. Roosevelt, Sarah Bernhardt, Queen of Hamburg—suggest an era when such thrift might have been necessary, rather than merely nutty.

Over the years, the house had fallen on hard times: it was divided into dorms during the Second World War, and later into an awkward

Peonies in full bloom, *Photograph © Richard W. Brown*

duplex with a swimming pool/duck pond, until it fell into foreclosure and attracted squatters who used the dining room as a billiard hall. But the peonies that rose up around it every June had been a perennial symbol of hope to the neighbors, who might otherwise have called the city inspector's office more often than they did.

"I always knew those peonies would help turn this place around," said a woman who walks by the house every day on her way to the bus. "They must have called to you."

They hadn't really.

It's not that I don't like peonies. In June, there may be nothing more beautiful than a big double-headed bloom, wet with dew and crawling with tiny ants. Every morning that first summer I went outside with clippers and cut great, heaping bouquets that I used to fill vases, then milk cartons, then drinking glasses, then stock pots. I finally floated the flowers on little ponds of water—in cereal bowls! I brought the peonies to dinner parties, sent them with the kids to preschool, and even palmed them off onpassing bike riders.

Since I was outmatched by their numbers, the flowers began to overwhelm their ridiculously slender stalks, keeling over in the sun. A hard summer rain sent them splaying with centrifugal force, as if a bomb had detonated in their centers. "The last rose of summer" doesn't come close to evoking the kind of ruined and rotting decay of a few dozen peonies past their prime.

"First thing," said the landscaper I'd called to consult about the problem, "you need to diversify."

So, one morning, very early, when I thought it was safe, I went out with a shovel.

"It stresses the roots to divide them in summer," said a neighbor who quickly materialized over my shoulder. "It would be a shame for the neighborhood to lose them. They've been here forever."

I backed away slowly, but word seemed to get around fast that I had attempted to unearth one of the sacred peonies. Pilgrims arrived almost daily to make sure the plants were safe in my care.

"Next spring, you've gotta stake 'em," said a man I'd never met before as he drove slowly past in his car. "That's the key to taking care of those guys."

"You know, people think that ants open the blooms, but it's not true," said a woman walking by with her dog. "They just like the taste, I guess. And aren't you lucky to have so much ant food!"

"Did you know those flowers have been here since at least the 1930s?" asked a woman who walks by every Sunday on her way to church. "They're heirlooms, I'm sure."

It seemed there was a concerted campaign to help me to see the beauty in these flowers, which by Independence Day looked worse than spent fireworks exploded over the driveway. Since there was plenty to do inside the house—did I mention it had been a flophouse?—I resolved

Peony detail, *The Illustrated Dictionary of Gardening*, circa 1900

to take care of the problem early the next spring, before anyone could stop me. But then there was an early thaw, and a birthday party a couple of doors down, and a kitchen conversation that turned, as it always seemed to when I was around, to gardening.

I kept my eyes lowered and hoped the neighbors would forget to ask me what my own landscaping plans were. They did not forget. Rather, they seemed intensely interested.

"Well," I answered, "I'm thinking of adding some hydrangeas, and maybe an azalea or two, and probably a little shade garden under the tree . . ."

"Sounds nice," someone said.

"Yep," I said, suddenly deciding to come clean. "And I'll probably have to ditch some of the peonies."

A hush fell over the room, which I quite naturally interpreted as censure. Probably they were considering whether to report me to the city inspector or the garden police. Clearly, we'd have to put the house up for sale. Then someone broke the silence with a request.

"Well then, I'll take dibs on the white ones," said one of my neighbors. "There's a spot right near the garage that would be perfect."

"And I've always loved the bright pinks," said another.

"Now, are they the Festivas, or the Bernhardts? I think I want the Bernhardts," said a third.

Suddenly, I understood what had been happening all along. These neighbors weren't preservationists intent on keeping everything the way it always was. They were gardeners who had spent long years just waiting for an owner willing to share. We wouldn't have to move after all— though we would have to spend a weekend in September parceling out the peonies to everyone who asked.

I now think of my friends with the rhododendron problem and wonder if they were too quick to transplant themselves to another neighborhood. In another season they might have learned the neighbors were not nearly so angry about ripping up that rhododendron, as they were disappointed it hadn't been divided and replanted on more familiar ground.

79

I've visited Tasha in all sorts of weather, both bad and brilliant, and even when her mountaintop is drenched with sun, the house seems dark inside. So the garden is particularly sparkling when you step out the door and find it stretched in front of you. While your eyes adjust, you can see only the nearest terrace, which unfolds like a pleasant dream in the depths of night. It seems surreal, like a splendid mirage, and sometimes I wonder if the house was made purposefully dark just to bestow the garden with that glistening effect.

—Tovah Martin, *Tasha Tudor's Garden*, 1994

*Chapter 3*

# Gardens of Lore

*Opposite:* Tasha Tudor's Garden, *Photograph by Richard W. Brown*

*Above:* Classic Watering Can, 1940 issue of *Vaughan's Gardening Illustrated*

# Tasha Tudor: Springs Eternal

*by Tovah Martin*

*A*uthor Tovah Martin first met Tasha Tudor when the acclaimed artist and gardener paid an unexpected visit to Logee's Greenhouses in Danielson, Connecticut, where Martin was the staff horticulturist. A friendship grew as Martin paid many visits to Tasha Tudor's famous gardens in Vermont to gather fodder for *Tasha Tudor's Garden* (Houghton Mifflin, 1994) and *Tasha Tudor's Heirloom Crafts* (Houghton Mifflin, 2000).

The two have kept in touch, and this past spring Martin wrote the following update on the garden, which was first published in the magazine *La Vie Claire*.

*Opposite:* Foxgloves in the Tudor Secret Garden, *Photograph by Richard W. Brown*

Spring is still magic at Corgi Cottage. With time's passing, the garden has just added patina. The fruit trees are lacier, the daffodil clumps denser, the whole scene flooded by an ocean of deep blue forget-me-nots like never before. And Tasha still tries to coax friends to come and visit, casting the lure of unleashed dianthus, now gamboling pell-mell throughout; or seducing you with tantalizing descriptions of Exbury azaleas, now upwards of 10 feet tall, wading among bluebells.

Getting there still requires going down a series of remote roads, each one a little bouncier than the street before. As civilization falls away, the farther fetched lanes are progressively less paved than previous routes leading to the weathered cottage. So by the time you pull in, reality has literally been left in the dust. When you arrive, the world slips into a surreal kaleidoscope of bleeding hearts, daffodils, tulips, and ancient crabapple trees in frothy blossom. The common denominator being the sea of forget-me-nots and Johnny-jump-ups (Tasha persists in referring to them as "ladies' delight," a common name conjured up by her childhood nanny, no matter that only relatives and a few initiated friends are privy to what she means) that swirl beneath your feet.

Corgi Cottage probably will forever remain a place of prevailing lushness, where nature—although not totally left to its own devices—is definitely having a lark. And yet, there's a suffusion that says the landscape has been intensively worked. It all comes out looking like a collaboration—as though the creeping phlox, daffodils, and crabapples all teamed up with Tasha to create the scene.

If it's warm, there will be tea on the back porch, with hand-woven antique tablecloth, linen napkins, silverware, and china. If it's chilly (and Tasha's slender frame feels a chill more readily than most), tea will be set up by the woodstove. No matter what, probably even if war was declared (especially if some crisis was trying to disrupt the foundations of polite society), Tasha would serve tea punctually at four o'clock. Some things never change, nor should they.

So there you are, trading tidbits on camellia or lily cultivars, in the midst of Tasha's antique linens, her ornate birdcages with twittering feathered things flitting around inside, all her vintage cooking utensils and recipe boxes poised for action, and Tasha will insist, if queried, that she doesn't collect. "I don't collect anything," she'll say with more than a hint of impatience in her tone and in that affirmative pitch that doesn't invite further discussion. Don't believe a word of it. She remains the most consummate collector I've ever met. At the moment, it's hyacinths and hollyhocks. Years ago it was crocus, reticulata iris, and species tulips, which brings us to the annual bulb order.

Every year, first week in October, the spring bulbs arrive. And I suspect that everyone secretly dreads the moment the box is discovered in the three-sided structure where the UPS driver has been bidden to leave parcels, rather than braving the road. Tasha probably doesn't do the planting nowadays. But I can't imagine that she leaves it totally in anyone else's hands—no matter how capable. Nowadays, several family members and friends do the heavy digging and other sundry garden drudgery ("Ah, you should meet my weeder—witchgrass trembles when she walks by"). No, she has scads of help, but nonetheless, she's definitely out there directing up a storm. Because when she put in her order for the thousand odd bulbs that arrive, Tasha had a destination in mind for each. And that's where they must go. Period. It has to do with subtle innuendos of color. ("I never think of color," she'll protest. But I've come to the conclusion that she designs subliminally.) Truth is, her eye is easily offended. As evidence, I submit the fact that every year she threatens banishment or at least relocation for a certain azalea that fails to mingle properly with its comrades. The red doesn't play well with its neighbors. Fortunately, it blooms briefly, its reign of

Burpee's Red Cup
Daffodils, 1934

85

terror only tormenting her eyes for a few weeks. And, although she claims that her mother was passionate for orange ("Mother being mad for Japanese art"), Tasha uses the color sparingly and advisedly, I've noticed, preferring peach (although that prejudice, also, she will not admit). But then, she will obstinately throw in some suffused glowing saffron crown imperial fritillarias, just to keep you guessing.

Perhaps the only thing that Tasha has never denied is being an artist. "But definitely not an *artiste*," she'll interject vehemently. It's a fine line. Although she refuses to categorize her style and she won't hear of comparisons with others who have wielded paintbrushes to the world's benefit, she admits that her time is mostly taken up dabbling with colors in front of an easel for better or worse. And that hasn't changed in the least. At the age of 90 (and Tasha is proud of and perfectly willing to publicize her vintage), she still has a standing room only crowd of ideas waiting to be tackled. But then, as long as I've known her, Tasha always has several projects on-going. Idle simply is not in her vocabulary, even if seniority might have earned her some leisure moments. She's every inch an artist, but won't entertain that her talent bestows an elevated understanding of anything. Well, actually, she'll allow that she's an exceptional cook—while usually splitting credit for her pies with the freshly ripened apples and laying hens.

So needless to say, she won't cabbage to the suggestion that she ever sat down and designed the garden. "It just grew, like Topsy," she insists. Of course, that really isn't the case. At one point or another, every garden had a plan—vague, perhaps, and definitely never committed to paper—but nonetheless, deep in the recesses of Tasha's mind, I'm sure she had a eureka moment governing each garden, and then carried it out (given the number of gardens on the property, it's clear that Tasha is struck with more frequently occurring eurekas than most of us).

Is there a common theme that recurs throughout her landscape, you might wonder? Well, yes and no. Being confined to a theme wouldn't sit well with Tasha. Certain gardens are dense with particular plants, although nothing is really dedicated solely to one subject. The foxgloves are primarily in the secret garden and there's a designated place where

Tasha's Peony Walk, *Photograph by Richard W. Brown*

most of the peonies grow. She doesn't do straight lines often, unless to follow a wall or hem a path, and even then, she lets rambunctious seedlings cut in. But if there is a theme, it is profusion. Tasha has always understood the value of using her entire canvas. The garden is a many-layered affair, and time has only added to the splendor, headiness and saturation of the scene on a very sensual level. She had the foresight to put in shrubs, trees and climbers early in the game. They're now more magnificent than ever. You can become lost in Tasha's kingdom more than any other garden I've experienced in my life. That spellbinding capacity hasn't diminished one iota. In fact, it's intensified.

Just as she will concede that her art has progressed over time ("Of course, out of necessity, my work has evolved. Everything changes"), the garden has also matured. Tasha's son, Seth, offered the observation during tea one day that Tasha's art has gained a certain softness. The garden has done likewise. And in it, Tasha permits only "what she likes." That said, she's fond of almost anything heirloom. Daylilies not making the cut, no matter how deep their roots. In the same spirit, she has never cottoned to gladiolus, poinsettias or wooly begonias. And she abhors double flowers—without exception: tulips, snowdrops, hollyhocks and fuchsias alike. It doesn't really matter how long a double flower has been in cultivation. Bad taste, after all, has run throughout history. In Tasha's estimation, double flowers in general should have been ditched ages ago. Single flowering tulips are superior.

And she has been somewhat crimped by the weather, the weather remaining one of Tasha's dearest topics. For as long as I've known Tasha (and we do go back some), every year has been "unique"—tolerated, perhaps, like an unusual child, but also the subject of speculation and discussion concerning its petulance. "This has been a most abnormal season," she'll declare. "The whole year has been odd," she'll observe. But then, year after year has weighed in on the strange side. That being the case, she judges the degree of a year's adversity in direct proportion to whether the heirloom roses burst forth with the desired vigor or if the Darwin tulips are ruined by rainstorms. She will hope that it is a good apple year or a season conducive to her new penchant for hollyhocks. Don't misunderstand: she doesn't begrudge Vermont its ferocious winters. Far from it. Tasha revels in snow and only frets when the white stuff is lacking. As for summer, it's ten degrees cooler on her mountain crest than in the depths of town. But when a season smites her primroses, she's understandably incensed. And her favorite flowers (although she's not quick to pledge allegiance to any plant) remain the forget-me-nots and Johnny-jump-ups (okay, "ladies' delight") that soldier on no matter what.

Which brings us back to the spring bulbs. Because they can't be flummoxed by caprices in weather. Vermont can by as whacky as it wants weatherwise, and the hyacinths will happen. Ditto for the daffodils. Even though Tasha claims to thrive on winter, she probably wouldn't be so keen on umpteen feet of the fluffy wet covering if it weren't followed by a surge of spring flowers. Winter, in Tasha's eyes, is the necessary preparation prior to primroses, snowdrops and all good things. But not to take any chances, Tasha plants bulbs by the hundreds, purchases pansies by the crateful (and yet, is infinitely finicky about which pansies are permitted on the premises). So that spring proclaims victory by sheer mass. I don't doubt that Tasha harbors a fondness for winter. But I do believe she admires spring more.

Spring at North Hill, *Photograph by Joe Eck*

# The Visitors

*by Joe Eck*

*T*he names Joe Eck and Wayne Winterrowd, both landscape designers, have become synonymous with their garden at North Hill, five beautiful acres of land filled with more than 5,000 species of flowers and plants near Readsboro, Vermont. Publication of their book *A Year at North Hill: Four Seasons in a Vermont Garden* (Owl Books, 1996) introduced their famous garden to a wider audience, although by that time gardening enthusiasts already had been making annual pilgrimages to North Hill for seven years. In the following piece, Eck writes about the experience of opening the private garden to the public. Joe Eck is also the author of *Elements of Garden Design* (North Point Press, 2005).

For the past seventeen years, North Hill has been open to the public three times each summer—the last day of June, July, and August—as a charitable benefit for the AIDS Project of Southern Vermont. At first it was a simple affair. Anyone who wished could drive up, park on the road, drop a voluntary contribution in the basket, and stay as long as they liked. Visitors were mostly local, though that word is only loosely applicable in rural Vermont, where few places are close to each other. They came from surrounding towns—Brattleboro, North Adams, and Bennington—and usually they were friends or friends of friends. If anyone arrived from Montpelier or Burlington, they had made a real effort to get here, and we appreciated that. At the end of each day, contributions might total $300 or $500. Anything higher than that was cause for jumping about and shouting.

But as the garden expanded in size (to the point that the late J. C. Raulston said, "It will eventually implode on itself, like the universe") and its reputation grew, more and more people came, even from as far as New York City. We didn't flatter ourselves, because Vermont is a lovely place, and gardeners began planning little vacations around our Open Days, another among the many reasons to visit Vermont. More and more frequently we began to get questions like, "Is there a nice place to have dinner around here?" or "Can you recommend a pleasant B and B?," indicating that these visiting gardeners did not have a home to go to. Once, in those relatively early days, we were even startled by the question "Where does one go around here for a nice cream tea?" Clearly, our demographics had changed.

Other things also changed. Because the garden was a designation it seemed to need a name. From two centuries before we came to Readsboro, the part of the town we live in—or on—was called North Hill. So that is what we called our garden. North Hill is, after all, in the Green Mountains, and so our road is relatively steep. There is absolutely no parking anywhere, and certainly not within the garden itself. Cars would pile up halfway down the hill, a hard hike for most visitors, and certainly for elderly people. Our neighbors quickly recognized the parking as a nuisance, and we were gently admonished by the town

A garden room at North Hill, *Photograph by Joe Eck*

selectmen to find a solution. The garden had also begun to suffer. Most visitors arrived between the convenient hours of 10:30 and 2:30. The fieldstone paths that thread through the garden are narrow, so in stepping aside to allow others to pass, visitors might unwittingly tread on the one minute Corsican mint we had got to overwinter. One polite lady misjudged the edge of a paving stone and landed bottom first in *Rosa spinossima*. She simply could not have found a worse place to land.

So the AIDS Project decided on a ticket system that would limit the garden to 300 visitors a day, and also assign times, usually the one requested, but sometimes on a take-it-or-leave-it basis. Parking was at the local school two miles below the garden, and a minivan ran shuttles every 15 minutes. This system turned out to be very good for the garden, as it limited the number of visitors and it controlled traffic, both within and without. It also turned out to be good for the Project, because the very fact that visitors had to secure tickets beforehand dramatically increased contributions. Each year since has been better than the year before, and in 2005, we topped $15,000 in three days, all from contributions that have remained strictly voluntary.

Most visitors are wonderfully appreciative, even embarrassingly so. Though we call ourselves elderly, as gardeners, at least, we are still capable of blushing, and we did just that when a lady clutched one of us by the arm and said, "I feel like I have just seen Monet's *Water Lilies* for the first time!" Even on our best days, when abundant sunshine has followed a nice gentle rain and all our weeding and staking is done, and when the whole garden smiles at us, we would never go so far as to say that. Nor would we say, as another visitor did when our flock of snow-white pigeons circled in clear blue air above us, "I think I just saw God fly over!" Still, we do appreciate compliments, most particularly on some plant we have struggled to make survive, or on an old specimen plant we ourselves have loved for years, summer and winter. Modesty seems to us one of the crucial attributes of a gardener, with so many failures in our face. But we are human, after all.

Tough-growing Alpines on a garden wall, *Photograph by Joe Eck*

Occasionally—not so often—there is the garden visitor whose essential pleasure in visiting gardens seems to consist in finding fault. They are sometimes very generous with their criticisms, and they say things like "You'd do better with your roses if you pruned a little more heavily," or "Lovely garden, but I do think there are too many hostas slathered about." Sometimes they have deep biases, and then they say, "I'd certainly like to see this garden without so many common annuals in it!" or "Aren't all these rhododendrons you have rather dreary in the winter?" Sometimes they are rank snobs, and wonder aloud, "Where are the vistas?" "Where is your swimming pool?" Once, weeding behind the bushes, we heard one elegant lady, looking at our small gray house, say to her friend, "Surely they don't LIVE here!" What we've so far never heard, however, is a departing visitor saying to an arriving one, "Turn around and go home, honey. It isn't worth the price of admission!" That's what a friend with a beautiful garden on Long Island was once told on an open day, when she went down to help with the parking.

Vintage seed packets for stocks, sweet pea, and aster, circa 1925

What we most dread are the self-proclaimed members of the environmental police, who are always experienced gardeners, and sometimes even declare themselves to be certified master gardeners. They are the ones who ask with seeming guilelessness, "Do you use chemical fertilizers?" or "I notice your lawns are free of weeds. . . ." They also always need to tell us that we are criminally negligent for having planted so invasive a plant as bamboo. "Bamboo simply *ruined* my sister's garden in Maryland!" But North Hill is in Zone 4 (-30 degrees Fahrenheit) where no bamboo in the world is likely to take over or even flourish without elaborate winter protection. These people also seem to reach boiling point when they see the beautiful *Iris pseudacorus*, grown here in many rare forms, including a pure white one we collected ourselves. "That is an invasive plant!" they say, pointing an accusing finger as much at us as at it. They would have passed whole swamps full of it on their way to us, but still they believe our little could add to the offending mass. We suppose in these cases it is the thought that counts most.

Opening one's garden to strangers is a curious experience in self-exposure, almost (God forbid!) like standing before them naked. We have certainly found that preparing for each of these days causes us to work off the garden's flab, tending to many small areas that cumulatively would result in something like horticultural cellulite. It's a drill, and the next-to-last thing we do is crisp the edges, because, as the late Sir David Scott remarked, "When visitors are expected, edge, don't weed." At the very end, we sweep all the paths, which, after so much frenzy, is a steady soothing motion that gives us the feeling we are ready. We hope our visitors see the difference, but we certainly do, and it is only because of Open Days that we can have that rarest of pleasures gardeners can experience, the sense that the garden is as close to perfect as we can possibly make it.

There are other benefits as well. One is that on three days of the best part of the gardening year, you can appear completely at ease and totally hospitable. Because we are very private people, and also because we must still earn a living, (and probably always will), our idea of

Summer at North Hill, *Photograph by Joe Eck*

complete horror is a stream of visitors coming through at any old time. Of course, they are mostly nice people, and some are connected to someone we know, whose name they use, making us feel that if we turn them down we will have offended a good friend. Those are always the ones who say "We'll be arriving around 11:30, and can we take you to lunch?" As Readsboro is a village of around 350, approximately 45 minutes from any significant town, that simply means we will be cooking another summer lunch.

But for many years now, when we get the inevitable question after a lecture, "Is your garden open to the public?" we can answer with total sincerity, "Oh, yes! It is open on the last day of June, July, and August for the benefit of the Southern Vermont Area AIDS Project and you can make your reservations on line at www.AIDSProjectSouthernVermont.org. Contributions at the gate are strictly voluntary and are tax deductible." We have that bit memorized. And we sound both gracious and also committed to a wonderful cause. Which we are.

# Down the Garden Path

*by Beverley Nichols*

Prolific author Beverley Nichols (1898–1983) established himself as a gardening writer when he captured the renovation of his first garden at Glatton in his books *Down the Garden Path, A Thatched Roof,* and *A Villiage in a Valley.* In later years, Nichols wrote books about two other gardens, those that surrounded his Georgian mansion and the gardens at his Sudbrook Cottage. Those who read Nichols' books came to know his gardens intimately. The following excerpt first appeared in *Down the Garden Path,* published originally in 1932 and again by Timber Press in 2005.

*Opposite:* English wood hyacinth in a Northeastern garden, *Photograph* © *Richard Felber*

A narrow lane, that twists and turns, directs you from the Great North Road to the village of Allways. It is seldom that one meets any traffic on it. A startled child, pressing back into the hedge with exaggerated caution as you pass . . . a woman on a bicycle with a floppy, old-fashioned hat and a curved back . . . an occasional farm cart, which can only be passed with great ingenuity and many amiable sallies. For the rest, the only other occupants of the road are the rabbits, which are legion. In the spring there are many young ones, so pathetically innocent and silly that sometimes it is necessary to stop the car, dismount, and speak quite rudely to them before they are so obliging as to run away. At night their eyes glow with phosphorescent fire and sometimes they are hypnotized by the lights of the car, so that one must pull up, and turn out the lights, in order that they may recover their self-possession. Very pleasant are those little halts, in the dark, with the wind playing in the high trees above, and the rain dripping monotonously on the wind-screen.

There were rabbits in plenty on the day that the car rattled down the lanes towards my inheritance, but I was too excited to be over-anxious about their welfare. Though I had only spent a single weekend in this place that was now my own I remembered the country-side as clearly as if I had lived in it for many seasons. The flat, quiet fields with their ancient willows that would so soon be feathered with green . . . the wide, meandering stream by the side of the road . . . the coppice of beech and chestnut with catkins swinging in the breeze . . . .

And now, the familiar bend in the road, the glimpse of a thatched roof, the sudden view of the white walls sturdily timbered. And it was mine . . . mine!

I jumped out of the Ford. My hand trembled violently as I paid the driver. The car turned, shunted and drove away. For a minute I stayed there in the road, staring at this beloved thing. It was difficult to realize that it was mine, from the top brick on the chimney to the grass at the foot of the walls. No . . . right down to the centre of the earth, and up to the heavens above, it was mine. But one cannot grasp these things as quickly as all that.

Then, as I stood there, I again remembered the existence of Arthur. Surely it was a little odd that nobody had come to greet me? I stepped across to the house and tried the door. It was bolted. I knocked, and waited. Who *was* Arthur? What was he like? Somehow I had assumed, as a matter of course, that he must be perfect.

My meditations were interrupted by the sight of a curious figure in the hall. It was a man in black, with a pale suspicious face. He was peering at me. Then he came to the door and opened it.

"Arthur?"

"I was expecting you." His voice seemed to come from a very long way off. He spoke with a slight Irish accent.

It was on the tip of my tongue to say that if he was expecting me it was rather strange that he should not do something about it. However, I said nothing, partly because he had already glided away, leaving me with a suitcase in my hand, and partly because nothing could destroy the elation of these first few moments in my own home. I shut the door, kicked the suitcase against the wall, and went through to the front room. One had to stoop to avoid the low beams. My heart was beating very quickly, because now, at last, I was to see again the garden of which I had so often dreamed.

I stepped through the window. Stopped dead. Blinked . . . Looked again . . . and the spirit seemed to die within me.

It was a scene of utter desolation. True, it was a cold evening in late March, and the shadows were falling. No garden can be expected to look its best in such circumstances. But this garden did not look like a garden at all. There was not even a sense of order about it. All design was lacking. Even in the grimmest winter days a garden can give an appearance of discipline, and a certain amount of life and colour, no matter how wild the winds nor dark the skies. But this garden was like a rubbish heap. In my mind's eye there had glowed a brilliant bouquet of flowers. I cherished the memory of beds that had glowed like the drunken canvas of an impressionist painter. I recalled arches weighed down with their weight of burning blossom. Through my mind there still drifted the languid essences of July, a summer halo encircled me and . . .

And now? Nothing. Earth. Sodden grass. Rank bushes. A wind that cut one to the marrow. I shivered.

Then I pulled myself together. It was unreasonable, surely, to be shocked by this prospect. One could not expect summer glory in the middle of winter.

But this mood did not last for long. For it was *not* the middle of winter. It was the beginning of spring. One knew enough poetical tags to be aware that daffodils took the winds of March, that snowdrops had been

Plant Ferry's Seeds vintage advertisement, early 1900s

nicknamed the 'fair maids of February,' that more than one poet had chronicled the advent of the primrose. But here was no daffodil, no snowdrop, no primrose.

I pulled the collar of my coat up and strode into the garden. Everywhere, there was the evidence of appalling neglect. Ignorant as I was of all the technicalities, I knew, at least, that good gardeners did not leave the old shoots of pruned roses lying on the ground. The roses seemed to have been pruned in the autumn, and the cuttings left on the beds through the winter. Nor did good gardeners allow hedges to grow apace, nor let ivy trail up the stems of young trees, nor permit the paths and borders to be swallowed up by ugly weeds. Why—there were even old newspapers lying sodden in the orchard!

A garden bench among the roses, *Photograph © Richard Felber*

I was just turning over one of these newspapers with a stick when there was the sound of a footstep behind me. I turned and saw Arthur only a few paces away. How he had come so near without making any sound, I cannot imagine. Still, there he was. He had pale watery eyes, and drooping shoulders. He smelt strongly of gin. His hands hung straight down by his side.

"Oh . . . Arthur . . ."

"Yes sir?" He spoke as though he were drugged.

"The garden seems a little . . ." I paused. I am terribly bad at "telling people off"—especially if they are in a subservient position. So I concluded weakly ". . . there seems a good deal to be done here."

"There is, sir. Far more than one man could do by 'imself."

"I wouldn't say that."

"No sir, but then . . . you 'aven't 'ad much to do with gardens before, 'ave you?"

The sly insolence of the remark cut me. I looked him straight in his horrible watery eyes. I said:

"As far as I can see you haven't had much to do with gardens, either. At any rate you haven't had much to do with this one. . . ."

I will not humiliate either myself or the reader with a further recital of this discussion. There is always something a little degrading in the disagreements of master and man, or of mistress and maid. The dice are always loaded so heavily in favour of the employer.

I returned to the cottage, and drew the blinds. I wanted to shut it all out. I sat down and lit a cigarette. It was evident that a great deal of work lay before me.

Such was the garden, when I entered into my inheritance.

## Salvage

AND now the work of salvage began. There were tools to be ordered, a wheelbarrow to be bought, beds to be filled with roses, hedges to be clipped, bushes to be uprooted. The greenhouse had to be patched up, the tool-shed wanted a new roof. We had to decide on a place for a rubbish heap, to fix the limits of the kitchen garden. We had to rush

The Old-Fashioned Garden, *Photograph by Frances and Mary Allen*

Bill Whitney, tending his garden, *Photograph © Jane Booth*

about with quantities of manure, pushing it into the ground with a feeling of supreme benefaction. We had to get weed-killer (the non-poisonous sort), and sprinkle it on the overgrown paths. We had to leap with heavy hatred upon ants' nests and squash the brutes, which were over-running the whole garden. We had to burn, and destroy and ravage before we could really create. And the extraordinary thing about it was that gradually my impatient desire for immediate results, which is the besetting sin of all beginners, died down. I began to take a joy in the work for its own sake. Until you actually *own* a garden, you cannot know this joy. You may say 'oh yes, I love a garden.' But what do you really mean by that? You mean that you like to wander through rows of hollyhocks, swathed in tulle … (you, not the hollyhocks), and that you like to drink lemonade under a tree with a nice young man who will shortly pick you a large bunch of roses. You hope he will take the thorns off, and that there will not be any earwigs in them, because if you found an earwig on the rug in the car you would die with horror. (So should I.)

You like walking out on to a terrace and looking up at a wall that is covered with the pale, tipsy plumes of wistaria . . . to walk under arches of orange blossom, thinking the prettiest thoughts . . . and you may even stoop down to pick a bunch of pansies, if they match your frock. You like these things, yes.

But you do not like grovelling on the earth in search of a peculiarly nauseating slug that has been eating those pansies. You do not like putting a trowel under the slug, hoping that it will not suddenly burst or produce fearful slime, and tipping the slug with gratified horror into a basket. You do not like bending down for hours to pull up hateful little weeds that break off above the root . . . (not groundsel, because groundsel is a lovely weed to pull up) . . . but small docks and wretched things like that. You do not like these things, for one reason and only one reason . . . because you do not *own* the garden.

All gardeners will know what I mean. Ownership makes all the difference in the world. I suppose it is like the difference between one's own baby and somebody else's. If it is your own baby you probably quite enjoy wiping its nose. If it is somebody else's you would have to use a long pole with a handkerchief on the end . . . at least I should. That was why I loved all this early work, because the garden was the first thing I had ever really owned. It took ages to realize it . . . to this day the realization is not complete. I still stand before a hedge with a pair of shears in my hand, saying "I can clip this hedge exactly as I please. I can make it round or square or like a castle. If I choose, I can clip it away altogether, and nobody can arrest me."

To dig one's own spade into one's own earth! Has life anything better to offer than this?

Very soon, we shall be able to be far more definite, to deal with actual facts, to scatter hints, to tell stories with a certain amount of plot in them. But at the moment, I find, in writing this book, that I am up

Wonderful Dollar Collection of Delphiniums, *Deposit Seed Co.* catalogue, *1929*

against the same difficulty which confronted me when I wrote my first book. That was a school story called *Prelude.* It still brings me a large weekly correspondence from wistful boys in Colonial swamps.

The difficulty one has in writing a school story is that nothing ever happens at school. (Nothing, I mean, that one could possibly print in anything but a German Nature magazine.) Of course, there *are* school stories in which things happen with almost breathless speed . . . prefects forge cheques, large boys rescue small boys from burning buildings, and housemasters' wives are seduced by members of the lower school before they have had time to say "Jack" . . . which is the word they usually do say, in ever tenderer accents, as the story proceeds. However, nothing like that ever happened in *my* school, so that I had to content myself by drawing a pretty picture of the gradual burgeoning of my young soul. Perhaps that is why the masters at Marlborough still refer to *Prelude* as "scurrilous literature."

A garden is like a school . . . it is a place of youth perpetually renewed . . . it arouses the same loyalties . . . it teaches the same lessons. Yet nothing really happens in it. Nothing 'novelistic.' A delphinium does not suddenly leap out of the herbaceous border and explode. A lilac bush does not, without warning, make rude noises behind one's back. What I am trying to express is that I cannot begin it all with a flourish . . . I cannot tell you that I went out one night, wide-eyed, with my hands full of seed, and sowed it, and lo! in the morning there was a field of blood-red poppies. Nothing like that happened at all, and lo! it would be a blood-red lie if I ever suggested that it did.

The Garden Tour, black-and-white photograph, October 1938

Yet just as a school is a place of slowly-expanding minds, of quiet adolescent dreams, of the play and inter-play of sweet friendship, so is a garden, whose story must be told with the delicacy of a leaf unfolding, in a soft, sighing prose that has the rise and fall of blowing branches. A pretty task to set oneself! Especially since my very first job must be the inevitably dreary one of describing the topography of my garden.

Topography in a garden book corresponds to genealogy in a novel. The best genealogist in fiction was Anthony Trollope. He had a gift for making his readers take a deep breath, swallow, and then glue themselves to his early pages until they knew everybody's aunts, uncles, and cousins much better than they knew their own.

Would that I had this gift in such a book as I am writing! For I want you, so much to know the way the paths run, to be aware that you must bend your head under this bough to avoid the sparkling raindrops, and step high, on a dark evening, as you enter the little box garden, so that you may not trip up. I fear that the gift is not mine, so that in a moment we shall have to show you a plan of it all . . . and I think that a plan is as tiresome as a family tree. Yet, it is necessary. How, otherwise, can we make The Tour?

Let me explain. Whenever I arrive in my garden, I Make The Tour. Is this a personal idiosyncrasy, or do all good gardeners do it? It would be interesting to know. By Making The Tour, I mean only that I step from the front window, turn to the right, and make an infinitely detailed examination of every foot of ground, every shrub and tree, walking always over an appointed course.

There are certain very definite rules to be observed when you are Making The Tour. The chief rule is that you must never take anything out of its order. You may be longing to see if a crocus has come out in the orchard, but it is strictly forbidden to look before you have inspected all the various beds, bushes, and trees that lead up to the orchard.

You must not look at the bed ahead before you have finished with the bed immediately in front of you. You may see, out of the corner of

*From the House of Gurney:* Spring and Fall catalog, 1924

your eye, a gleam of strange and unsuspected scarlet in the next bed but one, but you must steel yourself against rushing to this exciting blaze, and you must stare with cool eyes at the earth in front, which is apparently blank, until you have made certain that it is not hiding anything. Otherwise you will find that you rush wildly round the garden, discover one or two sensational events, and then decide that nothing else has happened. Which means that you miss all the thrill of tiny shoots, the first lifting of the lids of the wallflowers, the first precious gold of the witch-hazel, the early spear of the snowdrop. Which recalls one of the loveliest conceits in English poetry, Coventry Patmore's line about the snowdrop.

*"And hails far summer with a lifted spear!"*

It would require at least sixteen thick volumes bound in half calf, with bevelled edges, to contain a full account of a typical Tour round any garden. There is so much history in every foot of soil. So one can only hurry through it very briefly, to get the main outlines, and then draw a plan.

You step through some French windows into a small square garden, bordered with hedges of clipped blackthorn. Through the arch at the end is another garden, consisting of two big herbaceous borders, and a little circular lawn beyond. This gives straight on to some quiet fields, dotted with elms and oaks.

To the right, through another arch is an orchard, across which I have cut a path, edged with deep herbaceous borders. Beyond the orchard there is a coppice of poplars and sweet briar which hides the kitchen garden.

That is really all, except that there is a little Secret Garden on the other side of the house. It is only the size of a large room, and it is cut up into six box-edged beds filled with roses, and one large flower border, against a white wooden wall.

All of which leaves you, no doubt, in the same state of confusion as you were before. However, it had to be done. After this excursion, we shall have some justification for christening the various portions of the garden.

First comes the FRONT GARDEN. This is a very obvious title. In fact, its obviousness is its only claim to respect. It sounds prim and solid, like the front parlour. Which is what I try to make it. I like the flowers in it to be very well behaved, very formal, like glistening china ornaments on the mantelpiece of a house-proud woman.

The part beyond the Front Garden, through the aforesaid arch, we will call ANTINOUS' GARDEN. For I forgot to mention that there stands, in the centre of the little circular lawn, a statue of Antinous. I don't like garden ornaments, as a rule, especially in a humble garden like mine. I have a horror of those leaden cupids who illustrate, so gruesomely, the ultimate horrors of Bright's disease in many suburban pleasaunces. I cannot bear those grim terra cotta pelicans that peer sharply from thickets of bamboos in the grounds of tasteless Midland persons. I am depressed unutterably by those horrible little German manikins which some people scatter over their properties . . . grouping them oh! so archly . . . popping out of the rhododendrons, or lifting their horrid heads from a lavender hedge.

My Antinous, I feel, is of a different class. He is very beautiful, in himself. He once stood in the garden of an old house in Bedford Square. He was covered with grime and his limbs seemed stained eternally. I saw him first after lunch on a grey day of February. After shameless hinting and ogling I persuaded my host that he was unhappy in London, that it was not rain trickling from his pale eyes, but tears, that his feet were weary for the green grass. My host agreed. He really could do nothing else. It was ordained.

Antinous arrived in a crate, and was set in the centre of the little lawn. And gradually the sweet country rain washed his limbs, and the wind played about him. From his tired, worn fingers the grime departed, and his perfect, lyrical shoulders began to glisten in the sunlight. Now he shines and sparkles. He is spotless. To see him when the snow is on the ground, when the snowdrops are pushing humbly at his feet, when the winter sky is silver, white, and blue . . . ah! that is to see man as a flower, yes, as a strange white flower.

There remains only the ORCHARD and the SECRET GARDEN, which need no christening.

Here, therefore, we can draw the plan.

**TOMATO**

JOHN BAER
POMEDORO GROSSO

**Card Seed.Co.**
FREDONIA, N.Y.

**CABBAGE**

DANISH BALLHEAD

**Card Seed.Co.**
FREDONIA, N.Y.

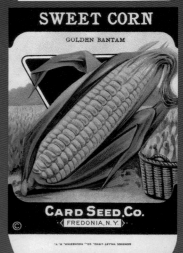

**SWEET CORN**

GOLDEN BANTAM

**Card Seed.Co.**
FREDONIA, N.Y.

**BEET**

EARLY BLOOD TURNIP

**Card Seed.Co.**
FREDONIA, N.Y.

**PEPPER**

LONG RED CAYENNE
PEPERONE

**Card Seed.Co.**
FREDONIA, N.Y.

**ONION**

LARGE RED WETHERSFIELD

**Card Seed.Co.**
FREDONIA, N.Y.

The first tomato of the season brings me to my knees. Its vital stats are recorded in my journal with the care of a birth announcement: It's an Early Girl! Four ounces! June 16! Over the next few weeks I note the number, size, and quality of the different tomato varieties as they begin to come in: two Green Zebras, four gorgeous Jaune Flammés, one single half-pound Russian Black. I note that the latter wins our summer's first comparative taste test—a good balance of tart and sweet, with strong spicy notes.

—Barbara Kingsolver, "Seeing Red," *Mother Jones* May/June 2007

*Chapter 4*

# Vegetable Heaven

*Opposite:* Vintage seed packets, Card Seed Company, Fredonia, New York

*Above:* The American Beauty radish, *The Maule Seed Book, 1932*

FARMER SEED AND NURSERY Co.
Faribault, Minn.
Season 1934
ANTICIPATION
MASTER FARMER
REG. TRADE MARK
"PRITCHARDS" — or SCARLET TOPPER
Newest Early Scarlet Globe Tomato
The outstanding variety for home garden or market. Fruits are large, smooth, globular, solid—with thick walls and few seeds.
Scarlet Topper is a heavy producer, disease-resistant and a good shipper. 75 days from setting of plants to marketable fruits.
Originated by Dr. Pritchard of the U. S. Dept. of Agriculture.
Pkt., 10c; ½ oz., 25c; oz., 40c; ¼ lb., $1.35. Prepaid.
See page 24.
REALIZATION

# The $64 Tomato

*by William Alexander*

Vegetables harvested from the garden have a freshness and fullness of flavor well above and beyond anything one can buy in a supermarket. But how does a homegrown tomato, for example, compare in price to one purchased at the local Piggly Wiggly? In this excerpt from the book *The $64 Tomato: How One Man Nearly Lost His Sanity, Spent a Fortune, and Endured an Existential Crisis in the Quest for the Perfect Garden*, published by Algonquin Books in 2005, William Alexander does the math, with surprising results.

*Opposite:* "Anticipation and Realization," *Farmer Seed and Nursery Co.* catalog, 1934
*Above:* Tomatoes for sale, *Photograph* © *Jane Booth*

Summer, like my tomatoes, was showing its cracks. A pre-back-to-school hush filled the school yards. The late-August nights were delightfully cooler, the days noticeably shorter, the afternoon shadows more angular. I watched a single rust-colored leaf blow across the garden the other day, a startling reminder of the passage of seasons, a hint of the winter to come.

But I still had tomatoes. Sweet, juicy heirloom tomatoes. I was in the garden, having just picked one of the few remaining Brandywines, when Anne came by and exclaimed, "What a beautiful tomato!"

"It should be," I joked lamely. "It probably cost us twenty dollars."

Anne looked at me, waiting for an explanation.

"We hardly got any," I said. "And we spent a lot on the garden this year."

"Surely you're exaggerating," Anne insisted, used to my hyperbole. I conceded that twenty dollars for one tomato was probably a gross exaggeration. But the exchange got me thinking.

Most of the gardeners I know don't garden to save money on groceries, although that might have been the norm a hundred years ago, when the backyard vegetable patch was a staple of most American homes. Most gardeners today garden because they enjoy the activity, or crave the freshness, or want vegetables, such as Brandywine tomatoes, that cannot be bought at the local Piggly Wiggly. Nevertheless it is reasonable to assume that it is cheaper to grow your own food than to buy it. That $1.79 pack of tomato seeds has the potential to feed a small community; most of us will use a half dozen seeds and throw out the rest, or use them next year. And the rest of the materials are free. You stir a little home-brewed compost into the vegetable bed, throw the seeds in the ground, add a little water, and presto, in a few months you have tomatoes, n'est-ce pas? Your initial $1.79 investment can return, I don't know, potentially fifty, a hundred, maybe even two hundred dollars' worth of tomatoes. Try to get a return like that on Wall Street.

But that isn't the total fiscal picture. I ran into a few expenses along the way before and after the ground was ready to receive those tomato seeds. Like building a garden. Like keeping the groundhogs and deer from eating everything in sight. This year seemed especially bad. I knew

I had put a lot into the garden this year and hadn't taken an awful lot out. So just for the heck of it, I decided I would try to figure out just what this "free" tomato really cost.

I started with the costs of building the garden (orchard excluded):

Garden design $300
Initial construction $8,500
Extra charge for stump pulling $300
Irrigation and drip hoses $1,100
Cedar edging $400
Electric fencing equipment
    (exclusive of charger) $400
Posthole digger $50
Posts for fencing $50
Two wrought iron gates and posts $400
Additional topsoil $250
Havahart trap $65
Velcro tomato wraps $5
Cedar for tomato posts $10
Steel edging $1,200
Labor for installation of edging $600
Forsythia border (including labor) $700
Gas-powered hedge trimmer for forsythia $75
Wood-chip mulch for forsythia $300
Chipper/shredder for shredding leaves for
compost $400
Dark bark mulch (fifty bags at $3 per bag) $150
Push lawn mower for lawn paths $80
Bag for lawn mower (never used) $40
Gas-powered lawn mower for garden $215
Garden books $100
Garden-magazine subscriptions $150
Peat moss and other miscellaneous soil additives $125
Removal of two trees $600

Alneer's Great Giant
Tree Tomato, *1947*
*Alneer Seeds* catalog

Not counting thousands of dollars of my labor thrown in for free, or yearly expenditures on seeds and seedlings, I ended up with the shocking figure of $16,565. When Anne and I started the project, we put what seemed to be a generous limit of $10,000 on it, and true to the Rule of Thirty-two (any home project will take three times as long to complete and cost twice as much as planned), we ended up over budget by 65 percent.

A bumper crop of beautiful heirloom tomatoes, *Photograph* © *Karen Melvin*

Of course, in doing my tomato valuation, I couldn't charge this all off against one year of gardening (only filthy-rich corporations with good tax lawyers could get away with that). Instead I amortized the cost of the garden over twenty years, by which time I would either be gardening somewhere else, not gardening, or rebuilding this garden. So to get the annual portion of the construction costs, I divided $16,565 by twenty years, yielding $828 per year. To this I added any additional expenses I incurred this year. As I have some expenses every year, I did not amortize them but charged them fully against this year's "profits":

When Tomato Seed is ordered at mail prices, and wished by express or freight, deduct 8c. per pound from catalogue prices.

## TOMATOES (Continued).

**LIVINGSTON'S ROYAL RED.** A grand new tomato. See page 13, this catalogue, for illustration and description. By mail, post-paid, pkt., 10c.; 3 pkts., 25c.; oz., 30c.; ¼ lb., $1.00; lb., $3.00.

**THE PONDEROSA.** See page 13, this catalogue, for description. By mail, post-paid, pkt., 10c.; 3 pkts., 20c.; oz., 25c.; ¼ lb., 75c.

**THE EVERBEARING.** See page 13, this catalogue, for illustration and description. By mail, pkt., 10c.; 3 pkts., 25c.; 8 pkts., 50c.

**EARLY DWARF CHAMPION.** In this variety we have a tomato of the best size and quality, growing on a strong, dwarf, upright bush, taking up little room, keeping the fruit well up off the ground, and producing enormous crops of splendid tomatoes of fine size, smooth and handsome appearance, as seen in above illustration. At the best stage on our trial grounds the past season, many plants produced over half a bushel of fine tomatoes. **The New Dwarf Champion** is a medium-sized tomato, just the right size for small gardens or close field planting. It ripens evenly, and we know of none more desirable. By mail, post-paid, pkt., 5c.; oz., 20c.; ¼ lb., 60c.; lb., $2.25. By express or freight, not prepaid, $2.00 per lb.

**Livingston's New Beauty.** Is a round, medium tomato, just the right size for canning and eating purposes. They are perfectly round, smooth as an apple, solid nearly to the core, with very few seeds, of the very best possible flavor, and ripen evenly all over. Their color is a beautiful deep red. By mail, post-paid, pkt., 5c.; oz., 20c.; ¼ lb., 60c.; lb., $2.00.

**THE PEACH TOMATO.** This is appropriately named, as the fruit resembles the peach in shape, and this resemblance is heightened by its distinct coloring and faint stripes from stem to blossom end. The tomatoes are two inches in diameter (see illustration above); color a deep rose and golden amber. For eating out of the hand it is without a rival. It is very productive, the fruits being borne in clusters of from four to eight. It is excellent for preserves; makes splendid pies. By mail, post-paid, pkt., 5c.; oz., 25c.; ¼ lb., 80c.; lb., $2.75.

**IMPROVED TROPHY.** Fruit very large and generally smooth, solid, good flavor and very productive; choice selected seed. By mail, post-paid, pkt., 5c.; oz., 20c.; ¼ lb., 75c.

**Red Cherry,** } Small fruited varieties. By mail,
**Yellow Pear-Shaped.** } pkt., 5c.; oz., 25c.

**THE MANSFIELD TREE.** This tomato originated in Wisconsin, and is one of the most satisfactory and valuable to plant in small garden, door yards, or where fowls of any kind are troublesome. The vine is a remarkably strong, upright grower, attaining the height of seven to eight feet in a very short time. The tomatoes are borne in abundance. **They are large, smooth, solid, and of most excellent quality.** By mail, post-paid, pkt , 5c.; oz , 25c.; ¼ lb., 75c.

**THE NEW STONE TOMATO.** This is another of Livingston's introduction. Of this we can speak from experience, having grown a large crop of them the past season **for seed purposes only.** We are compelled to say the **New Stone Tomato** far eclipses them all. This splendid tomato is just the right size (see illustration above). The skin is a dark red from stem to blossom end. No green spots to be seen around the stem; flesh bright red, very few seeds, **positively no hard core,** and of the best possible flavor. They ripen medium early and bear abundantly. By mail, post-paid, pkt., 5c.; 3 pkts., 20c.; oz., 25c.; ¼ lb., 80c.; lb., $2.75.

**TURNER'S HYBRID.** The foliage of the Turner Hybrid differs from all other varieties. It is a rank, strong grower, with thick stalks, and very productive. The fruit is fair size (see cut above), and solid. The average weight of the tomatoes is from 16 to 20 ounces. They ripen up evenly, and are entirely free from core. **Unequaled in fine flavor.** The form of the fruit is round, thick, smooth, firm, and solid; color a brilliant red. By mail, post-paid, pkt., 5c.; oz., 25c.; ¼ lb., 80c.; lb., $2.75. By express or freight, not prepaid, $2.50 per lb.

We are headquarters for **HOME-GROWN TOMATO SEED.** Special prices on large quantities.

Tomato varieties, *Wilson's Price List and Catalogue*, 1894

Holy smokes! I spent another $735 on the garden this year without even realizing it!

These costs plus this year's share of the one-time construction costs totaled $1,563. Now, since I was interested in the price of my tomato, I did not count everything that came out of the garden equally. I'm not even sure how one would do that. Instead I subtracted from the $1,563 the true market value (using the higher local farm-stand prices, not supermarket prices) of all the produce I harvested excluding Brandywine tomatoes. In the spirit of full disclosure, I should point out that this year was a terrible year for gardening (for me, anyway). We had record-setting high temperatures in July and August that decimated the lettuces and tomatoes, and I hadn't grown corn this year, further reducing my total yield. I don't usually weigh my vegetables (except potatoes, for some reason) as I bring them in from the garden, but judging by how many meals we got from our crops and how many jars of pickles we made, I was pretty well able to reconstruct the amount. But to be safe, I erred on the high side. Here is our yield:

Potatoes $45
Lettuce and mesclun $48
Squash $15
Cucumbers $15
Basil and other herbs $35
Sweet peppers $3
Sugar snap peas $30
Green beans $25
Cherry tomatoes $20
Leeks $48
Dona tomatoes $10
Strawberries $50

Henderson's Crimson Cushion Tomato, *Everything for the Garden* catalog, 1922

Representing $344 worth of produce, excluding Brandywine tomatoes. Now, $344 isn't exactly peanuts, but "gentleman farmer"? "Self-sufficient?" Who am I kidding? Three hundred forty-four dollars' worth seems like barely enough food to nourish the groundhog, let alone a family of four. In my meager defense, let me point out again that it was a very poor year (although, mysteriously, the local farm reported a great season); in other years we might be higher, but for this year we were stuck with $344. The other thing this reveals is that food is cheap. I actually grew a fair amount of food; it just wasn't worth much. For example, my local green market is selling a ten-pound bag of white potatoes for $1.50—just 15¢ a pound. A person could probably eat well from that buck-fifty bag for several days. (For this exercise I valued my Yukon Gold and fingerling potatoes at $1.50 per pound.) Every time I'm done picking sugar snap peas or rise from my stoop, aching, from picking green beans, I marvel that I can buy this stuff in the green market for a dollar a pound. How can anyone possibly grow green beans for a dollar a pound? I can't even pick them for a dollar a pound, it takes so long. It's a miracle that any farmer stays in business, but God bless them.

Back to my expensive tomatoes. Three hundred forty-four dollars (the value of this year's yield) subtracted from $1,563 left a cost of $1,219 for my stash of Brandywines. How many did I get this year? At the risk of making too many excuses, I'll point out that the heat just shut down my tomato plants in August. It is a known fact that heat before blossom set will shut down tomatoes, but I'd always thought that August heat was good for tomatoes. When I asked Doris at the farm if their tomato crop was as meager as mine, she looked at me as if I were crazy. They'd had a great tomato year, but they grow Big Boy and Roma tomatoes; perhaps these varieties withstand heat better than my purebred heirlooms. Or maybe the fact that they mulch heavily kept the roots cooler and the plants more productive. Or maybe they're just better farmers than I am. After all, they've been doing it for generations.

I know, I'm stalling. So just how many tomatoes did I get this year? Exactly nineteen. The groundhog got almost as many. They were large and delicious, these nineteen Brandywines, and that number does represent a tomato a day for almost three weeks. Still, it doesn't seem like much. It isn't much.

Time, finally, to do the depressing math: $1,219 divided by nineteen equals—gulp —$64 per tomato.

Holy cow.

This was sobering. I never realized how much growing my own food was costing me. I went to Anne with the numbers.

"You won't believe this," I said. "Remember that joke I made about the expensive tomato?"

"Uh-huh," she said, distracted, as she leafed through the New England Journal of Medicine.

"Twenty dollars turned out to be a tad low. That was a sixty-four-dollar tomato."

"Maybe that one you stuffed with crabmeat? That was good," she said, not looking up.

"You don't understand. I'm not talking dinner-menu prices. Every Brandywine tomato we picked this year literally cost us sixty-four dollars to grow."

Now I had her attention. She put the journal down and stared at me for what seemed an eternity.

"And just how do you know that?" she finally inquired hesitantly, not sure she really wanted to know.

I laid the spreadsheet in front of her. She studied it for a minute.

"We spent all this on the garden?"

"Maybe more. I'm sure I forgot some things."

She pushed away the paper as if it were contagious and flipped a page in her journal. "Well, we see this," she said, borrowing a phrase she often uses with patients. Meaning, in this case, that she was over the shock and ready to move on. And inviting me to join her. Truthfully I wished I hadn't done this exercise in accounting. Some things you're better off not knowing. I've said that the garden had become a family member, but at the moment it felt, not like the beloved grandmother you care for, but like the embarrassing uncle you avoid at weddings, loud and extravagant beyond his means, always in trouble, always in debt.

We see this. I, too, wanted to move on, but there was still one unspoken question troubling me, one that spanned months, years, ages. A question I both had to ask and was afraid to ask.

"Was it worth it?"

Anne deliberately closed the journal, placed both hands on the cover, and looked up at me.

And smiled.

KFNF
*Henry Field Speaking*

SPRING
1930

*Description and Prices
of Flowers and Vegetables
illustrated on this page
at bottom of page 1*

# Henry Field's SEED BOOK

1930 SHENANDOAH, IOWA, U.S.A. 1930

# Vegetables Again

*by Lee May*

After many years of growing ornamental plants and herbs, author Lee

May returns to vegetable gardening in his essay "Vegetables Again." A

regular gardening columnist for the *Atlanta Journal-Constitution* for many

years, May is also the author of two books, *Gardening Life* (Longstreet

Press, 1998), in which this piece was first published, and *In My Father's*

*Garden* (Deep South Books, 2002).

*Opposite: Henry Field's Seed Book,* Spring 1930

Pretty soon we took a stroll, to see what he was
having to water. I was amazed at how orderly
was his garden, rows straight and clean
as arrows ... the sundrenched garden grew just
about everything a family might need.
Collards, corn, butter beans, peas, tomatoes,
peppers, squash, watermelon, potatoes.
And, amazingly, peanuts, their vines twirling
out of a network of old car tires.
Proudly, my father pointed out each crop,
giving me a rundown on its progress,
how well he expected it to bear.

—Lee May, *In My Father's Garden*, 1995

In this year's first blushes, promise springs eternal. This is the year I keep a vow to my father and myself; I'll be growing food again.

Not enough to get me on any lists of biggest crops or biggest specimens, but at least enough to provide us a few good eats and save us from store-bought tomatoes.

It has been well over a decade since I grew anything to eat, other than herbs, and my father has never understood why I would use valuable ground to grow shrubs, trees, and perennials.

In his garden in Meridian, Mississippi, he has grown some serious food, including corn, beans, greens, peas, okra, squash, tomatoes, grapes, and peanuts. Eating from his garden is always a soulful treat.

At the end of one of our visits last year, my father dug out a little can from his tool shed and carefully picked from among his dried seeds some for me, making a starter kit: okra and watermelon seeds, peanuts, kernels of corn.

"You can get a good crop out of these," he said, as he handed me the container.

State Fair Watermelon 95 lbs.,
*The Henry Field Catalog, 1924*

Cuban Queen Watermelon Seeds,
Card Seed Co., early 1900s

Recently, I've been looking at the can. It's white cardboard, with a red plastic top, labeled Food Club sun-dried California raisins, and it is stamped, "Sell by February 25, 1993."

Well, I'm not sure when I'll plant the seeds, and I'll not be growing peanuts, corn or watermelons among the nandina, pieris, and bamboo. But the okra seeds will go into the ground. And I'll buy a few more seeds or seedlings to grow eggplant, peppers and tomatoes. Maybe as the season goes along, some others will inspire me. Many readers have been inspiring and encouraging since I wrote about my father's garden last June, including Seiho Tajiri, Gerald Wade, and John Yarbrough. They good-naturedly cajoled me to honor my father's wish—grow food.

"Steal a little space from your ornamentals and plant a little Ples Mae (my father's name) patch in your back yard," Yarbrough wrote in a note from Gainesville, Georgia.

Yellow plum, cherry, and standard-size tomatoes,
grown by Jane Booth, *Photograph © Jane Booth*

OK, this is the year. Tips and advice are welcome.

When we talked on the telephone the other day, my father did not seem surprised to learn of my promised garden, and I did not bother to tell him that part of the way I convinced myself to grow food was to contemplate the beauty of some vegetable plants.

The eggplant, for example, grows a wonderful rich purple, and peppers, in addition to satisfying my addiction to spices, give a space great reds, yellows, and greens. The foliage on both is attractive, too, as are okra's blossoms.

Perhaps I need not tell my father any of this. All along I've assumed he was growing food just for his stomach. Maybe it was for his eyes, too.

In any case, when we talked the other day, it was mostly about the advantages of growing our own: big flavor and little pesticide. "When you go to the market and pick up something, you don't know what you're getting," he said. "Even the store people don't know what's in it."

I'm not sure if he ever ate a store-bought tomato, and if this year's effort works out, I never intend to again.

There is some symmetry to my growing food again. The last time I did was when I lived in Atlanta in the 1970s, planting an ambitious garden that was much like my father's, including corn, beans, squash, tomatoes.

I recall harvesting maybe three ears of corn, and the other crops bore pitifully little, as the spot I chose was not nearly sunny enough.

Fortunately, there's more sun in my garden these days, as there is in my life.

As for my eighty-four-year-old father, he sounded sunny and strong the other day, probably stronger than he is. He gardened almost none last year, blaming failing health and vagaries of weather.

But, perhaps buoyed by the spirit of resolve that flows so heavily this time of year, he looked ahead to planting and, characteristically, lauded the hard work and reward connected to it.

"Nothin's gonna come and get in your lap," he said. "You got to work for it."

And he shared a bit of wisdom that I must remember as I rejoin the ranks of vegetable people: "It's a risky run any way you go. Always be prepared to go back over it again if you mess up; if you fail, just plant again."

*January 7, 1994*

A Bountiful Harvest,
*Photo used courtesy of Glenbow Archives*

RADISHES AND LETTUCE FOR SUMMER SOWING

SCARLET
TURNIP
WHITE TIP

VICKS
SCARLET
GLOBE

LONG
SCARLET
SHORT
TOP

WINTER
RADISH
CHINESE ROSE

RADISH
BURPEE'S
WHITE
DELICIOUS

ICICLE

LETTUCE
BUPPEE'S
WAYAHEAD

# Gardening in the Supermarket

*by Wayne Winterrowd*

*I*n the following essay, renowned garden designer Wayne Winterrowd provides a few ideas on how vegetable gardeners might entertain themselves through those long winter months. Wayne Winterrowd and Joe Eck have been nurturing their garden at North Hill, near Readsboro, Vermont, for more than twenty years. Winterrowd is the author of *Annuals for Connoisseurs* (Macmillan, 1996) and *Annuals and Tender Plants for North American Gardens* (Random House, 2004). With Joe Eck, he has written *A Year at North Hill: Four Seasons in a Vermont Garden* (Owl Books, 1996) and *Living Seasonally: The Kitchen Garden and the Table at North Hill* (Henry Holt and Co., 1999).

*Opposite:* "Radishes and Lettuce for Summer Sowing," *Burpee's Offering,* 1917

All gardeners enter any space or situation with an eye to what they could grow or use in their gardens. So I don't enter any supermarket without first sizing up the carrots. They are, of course, in the produce section, where hopes and expectations are highest. I may never make another carrot cup, but *I remember how to do it.* Even so, there may be other things calling to me if they look right and I have returned to that mood of childhood when the word "experimenting" included just about everything one did. Everyone knows how to sprout an avocado seed by sticking it with three toothpicks and suspending it in a jar with its base just touching water. If it is an avocado seed that is internally prepared to sprout, it will send forth a lusty shoot. You then pot it up, seed and all, and it burdens you with an ever-larger houseplant until it gets too heavy and you let it freeze at the end of its summer vacation on the patio. Sweet potatoes can also be stuck with three tooth picks and suspended that way, though in their case, the pretty vines that sprout can be cut with a bit of flesh and actually transplanted into the garden, where they will make even prettier vines, and—if you live in Zones 7 to 10—some sweet potatoes actually worth cooking and eating. It is good to know that a lump of real charcoal from the fireplace or the outdoor grill, well-rinsed and placed in the jar, keeps the water fresh and clear. (That was explained to me in *Fun for a Rainy Day.*)

Any lusty pineapple top could sprout into a fine houseplant, looking like an expensive florist's bromeliad (to which family it actually belongs) if you slice it off with about a half inch of flesh below the funnel of leaves, and bury that in free-draining compost. If you get fresh leaves from its top, after a year or two you might try putting a supermarket apple next to your plant and wrapping it up in a plastic bag salvaged from there, too. The ethylene gas from the apple may cause the pineapple to produce a single fruit at its top, for that is how it is done, essentially even in the fields of Hawaii, though the ethylene is synthetically produced, and not from apples.

Beyond these familiar experiments, the produce section of any supermarket offers other opportunities. I have always wondered, for example, whether a bag of carrots past prime and showing fine, white,

Maule's Blood Turnip. *The Maule Seed Book, 1932*

root hairs would produce umbels of Queen Anne's lace, if you bought and planted them in the spring. For all supermarket carrots claim descent from their wild progenitor, *Daucus carota*, the familiar and much-loved Queen Anne's lace of fields and roadsides. The great French nurseryman, Villemorin, found that from a common carrot he could breed back to Queen Anne's lace in a mere three generations. Carrots are biennial, after all, which means that they form leaves and roots the first year of their life and flowers and seed the second. The same is true of beets. So by planting beets from the supermarket in spring, you could theoretically get beet seed the next year. Beet seed is available, and the flower is not all that pretty. Still, it is a thing to keep in mind when push comes to shove, and we are reduced to cultivating our own cabbages.

Within the produce section of the supermarket, there are other things that offer promise to a gardener. A really fresh bunch of water cress, for example, will either show fine, white roots at the base of each stem, or promise to make them once you get home. All it needs is a pot of good rich dirt and some flowing water. You could keep your pot in a sunny window near the kitchen sink and flood it every day, or if you have a very sunny extra bathroom with a toilet under the window, you could take the lid off the tank, submerge the pot, and flush frequently. Your special pot roast, garnished with watercress from the guest-room toilet, might seem a little odd, even to close family. But gardeners often go to great lengths, and they keep their secrets. Their families also know that they are quite mad.

But in the produce section of the supermarket, we are not near finished. So in the fall—either late September or early October—you can weigh pods of garlic in your hand, and if they are plump and full, take some home to plant in the garden, either divided as single cloves or whole. You might then produce garlic to weave next year into braids and hang from the ceiling for your winter stews, but green garlic is really the point of this exercise. Nothing is quite like it when it is placed in strips over homemade pizza, or in so many dishes in Indian cuisine. In fact, we treasure it so much that we grow a few plants in pots on sunny windowsills throughout the winter. Scissoring them down for the Sunday pizza is always a little painful, since they are so green and pretty and full of life. So we approach them just as the Walrus and the Carpenter do in Lewis Carroll's famous poem, and can say that we "have eaten every one."

Within the same family, that bundle of green onions, so limp and wan and tightly constricted by its rubber band—kept to an illusion of freshness by a timed mist that turns them mushy—may nevertheless be some good variety of bunching onion, probably of Japanese breeding. If you can buy them in early spring and plant them almost anywhere in full sun, you'll have more green onions, half of which you can eat and the other half you can plant back in the ground. The seed of such stock, which is almost always produced by healthy plants, is worth sowing in late summer, for a spring crop of scallions. In the dead of winter, you could even pop the whole bunch into a 6-inch pot on a sunny windowsill, perhaps next to your garlic, producing a bunch of onions that might taste fresher than they did from the super-market sauna.

And now that gourmet potatoes are readily available, a handful of Russian bananas or Rose Finn apples can always be tucked aside in a paper bag to sprout and be planted out in the garden, come spring. Just be sure to wash them well with ordinary dishwashing liquid, on the chance they have been treated with a growth retardant. Then rinse them in a gallon of fresh water into which you have put 3 tablespoons of household bleach to eliminate any fungus or diseases they may carry. If you are *really* thrifty, you will cut each potato into sections with at least one eye, or growing tip, per

Purple Peruvian and Dark Red Norland Potatoes, Bill Whitney's Cape Cod garden, *Photograph* © *Jane Booth*

section and dry out the pieces for a day or two on the kitchen counter before planting them. Or, since growth is thickest at one end of the potato, the "rose end," you will plant only that and eat the rest.

So much for the living. Now for the inert. When I buy onions, I save every plastic mesh bag they come in, because one of them crumpled in the bottom of a pot to cover the drainage hole makes a perfect seal to keep soil from leaking out when houseplants are re-potted, while at the same time ensuring good drainage. In the case of quite shallow pots, such as those used for paper-white narcissus or bonsai trees, the mesh bags take a fraction of the space required by conventional pottery shard, thereby giving more room for sustaining roots. It is always well worth putting by a few of these bags to hang onions harvested from the garden in autumn, or potatoes, or dahlia tubers and gladiolus corms. There, mice cannot get to them, and good air circulation prevents the rotting that can be such a disappointment, come spring.

Long barbecue skewers are always to be treasured for staking, since so many plants—annuals and perennials—topple just about 6 inches above soil level. It is good to buy those long before you need them and leave them out in the weather for a month or two. Then they are not the toothpick yellow they come as, but a nice weathered gray. The red lids covering coffee cans, or the clear plastic ones from deli olives, fit just nicely under clay pots on the windowsill. And the generous, clear plastic domes that cover many vegetables in winter— particularly hydroponically grown lettuce—make wonderful little

Burpee's Early Flowering Sweet Peas, *Burpee's Offering*, 1917 greenhouses in which to start seedlings or root cuttings, if you remember to punch plenty of drainage holes in the bottom with a heated ice pick. Even a box of old-fashioned kitchen matches is always worth adding to your cart, because many garden plants, particularly peppers and eggplants, love extra phosphorus, and so the old gardener always buried a few match heads under their roots.

All these things are homely and familiar, but a keen gardener of whatever age will always take pleasure in discovery and experiment. So my most exciting forays into supermarkets recently have been into those that cater to Asian, Indian, or Central and South American customers. The vegetable bins in such markets offer a whole new world of possibilities, both for the cooking pot and the clay one. Most wonderful—so far—are elephant ears, either *Xanthosoma* or *Colocassia*. You can buy both from bulb catalogs, but it is more fun to buy them in the supermarket, and there you pay by the pound. But they will not be advertised as elephant ears. You must look for the names malanga, yautia, cocoyam, eddo, tannia, or sato-imo. You'll get elephant ears from all of them, but some will be purple, some the familiar green, and some will be stunningly huge. Start them in good clean humus-rich soil, in pots kept always moist and preferably placed on the furnace or radiator, where they're sure to get the bottom heat they love. When the elephant ears show signs of growth, move them to a sunny windowsill until all danger of frost is past and then transplant them into the garden.

I do not think supermarkets are a gardener's heaven, but maybe they are an anteroom, especially in the dead of winter, when the possibility of growing anything has deep appeal. And if I do ever get to Heaven, probably I will go straight to that celestial supermarket in the skies, where there must be possibilities I never dreamed of. For the time being, however, Stop & Shop serves well.

Choosing among flowers may be like choosing among children; each has its delights. But roses are the main flowers I bring indoors. My passion for roses borders on obsession. I have 120 rosebushes, and I feel that if I were to count them every day, *that* would be an obsession. I tell myself that at the moment it's just a hungry penchant allowed to run wild. Even though I have a splendid array of rosebushes, I keep buying more. I can't resist a healthy, heavily budded rose, and I rarely let the blooms stay on the bushes. The second they're ready to pick, I bring them indoors for arrangements.

—Diane Ackerman, *Cultivating Delight*, 2001

*Chapter 5*

# Ode to a Flower

*Opposite:* Climbing Roses, Garden of Gloria Eustis, *Photograph* © *Jane Booth*

*Above:* Rosa Gallica, *The Illustrated Dictionary of Gardening*

# Into the Rose Garden

*by Michael Pollan*

Award-winning author Michael Pollan ruminates on the allure and beauty of old roses in his essay "Into the Rose Garden," which first appeared in his book *Second Nature: A Gardener's Education* (Atlantic Monthly Press, 1991). Pollan is a professor of journalism at Berkeley and executive director of *Harper's Magazine*. His articles have appeared in the *New York Times Magazine*, *Harper's Magazine*, and *Smithsonian* magazine, and he has authored two other books: *The Botany of Desire: A Plant's-Eye View of the World* (Random House, 2002) and *A Place of My Own* (Delta, 1998).

After only a few days the buds reddened and swelled, and by the end of two weeks the canes had unfurled around themselves a deep green cloak of leaves, paler, daintier, and in finish more matte than the high-gloss foliage of modern roses. I had read that most old roses flower on "old wood" (last season's growth), so I had no expectation of blooms that first season. But in late June, after a month of rapid growth, Madame Hardy sent forth a generous spray of buds.

I had by now read so much about old roses that I frankly doubted they could live up to their billing. But Madame Hardy was beautiful. From a small, undistinguished bud emerged a tightly wound bundle of pure, porcelain-white petals that were held in a perfect half-globe as if by an invisible teacup. The petals were innumerable yet not merely a mass; more ladylike than that, the fine tissue of Madame Hardy's petals was subtly composed into the quartered form of a rosette, and the blooms made me think of the rose windows of Gothic cathedrals, which had not before looked to me anything like a rose.

It was hard to look at Madame Hardy plain, hard not to think her as an expression of another time—which of course, as much as being an expression of nature, she is. Though Madame Hardy did not appear until 1832 (bred, you'll recall, by Josephine's rose gardener and named for his wife), she embodies the classic form of old roses, and comes closer to the image the word rose has conjured in people's minds for most of Western history than does the rose in our florist shops today. When Shakespeare compared his love to a rose, this must have been pretty much what he had in mind. To look closely at the bloom of an antique rose is, at least in some small way, an exercise of the historical imagination: you see it through your own eyes, yet also through the eyes of another time. What an odd thing, though, for a rose is not a poem, or a painting, but a flower, part of nature: timeless. Yet, man in some sense made Madame Hardy, crossed and recrossed it until it reflected his ideal of beauty—and so today in my garden it reflects the sensibility of another time back at me. The rose is part of nature, but also part of us. So much for the mind of winter.

Salzer's Sunshine Collection, *John A. Salzer Seed Co.*, 1902 catalog

Admiring the beauty of Madame Hardy, I began to see why she should so excite rosarians of a snobbish bent—and to accept the slightly uncomfortable fact that, at least in the war of the roses, my own sympathies were not with the party of the people. Compared to modern roses, Madame Hardy is indeed an aristocrat, incomparably more subtle and, in form, so much more *poised.*

Once you have grown roses, you can begin to understand why people might project metaphors of social class onto them. Each bush itself forms a kind of social hierarchy. Beneath Madame Hardy's bud union is the rootstock of another, tougher variety—not a hybrid but a crude species rose, some hardy peasant stock that can withstand bad winters, but whose meager flowers interest no one. The prized hybrid is grafted onto the back of this anonymous rootstock, which performs all the hard labor for the rose, working the soil, getting its roots dirty so that the plant may bloom. The prickly shrub itself is not distinguished particularly, but it too is necessary to support the luxury of the bloom—its great mass of leaves manufactures the food, and its branches form the architecture without which flowering would not be possible. And the extravagant, splendid blooms, like true aristocrats, never seem to acknowledge the plant that supports them, or the fact that their own petals were once mere leaves. They comport themselves as though their beauty and station were God-given, transcendent. You cannot discern in the bloom of a rose the work of the plant, the sacrifice of its chafer-eaten leaves, the stink of the manure in which it is rooted. Roots? Madame Hardy asks, ingenuously. What roots? But if Madame Hardy calls attention to her pedigree, Maiden's Blush, the alba I planted beside her in my garden, seems to press her sexuality on us. Her petals are more loosely arrayed than Madame Hardy's; less done up, almost unbuttoned. Her petals are larger, too, and they flush with the palest flesh pink toward the center, which itself is elusive, concealed in the multiplication of her labial folds. The blush of this maiden is not in her face only. Could I be imagining things? Well, consider some of the other names by which this rose is known: Virginale, Incarnata, La Séduisante, and Cuisse de Nymphe. This last is what the rose is called in France where, as Vita Sackville-West tells us, blooms that blush a particularly deep pink are given the "highly expressive name" of Cuisse de Nymphe Émue, which she demurs from translating. But there it is: the thigh of an aroused nymph.

No, Maiden's Blush is certainly not the kind of old lady I expected when I planted roses. Her concupiscence, in fact, has made me wonder if all the baggage with which the rose has been loaded down might be just a cover for these nymph thighs, for this unmistakable carnality. For though Maiden's Blush bears an especially Provocative bloom, every one of the old roses I planted, and all the ones I've since seen and smelled, have been deeply sensuous in a way I wasn't prepared for. Compared to the chaste buds and modest scent of the modern roses, these old ones give freely of themselves. They flower all at once, in a single, climactic week. Their blooms look best fully opened, when their form is most intricate; explicit, yet still so deeply enfolded on themselves as to imply a certain inward mystery. And their various perfumes—ripe peaches, burnt almonds, young chardonnays, even musk—can be overpowering.

*Rosa Bonica,* Hedda Kopf's garden, Woodbridge, Connecticut, *Photograph* © *Jane Booth*

More even than most floral scents, the fragrance of these roses is impossible to get hold of or describe—it seems to short-circuit conscious thought, to travel in a straight line from nostril to brain stem. Inhale deeply the perfume of a bourbon rose and then try to separate out what is scent, what is memory, what is emotion; you cannot pull apart the threads that form this . . . this *what?*

By the time all my old roses had bloomed I had begun to think that maybe Marx has less to tell us about the world of roses than Freud. Certainly Freud would assume that anything we have invested with this much significance must exert some powerful sexual pull. I returned to my rose literature, and surely enough, the same rosarians whose prose had seemed to bristle with class consciousness now read to me as slightly sex-crazed. Would it be disrespectful to suggest that Graham Stuart Thomas, O.B.E., V.M.H., D.H.M., V.M.M., has a thing for old roses? Here is his full description of Madame Hardy: "There is just a suspicion of flesh pink in the half-open buds, emerging from their long calyces, and the flower open-cupped, rapidly becoming flat, the outer petals reflexing in a most beautiful manner, leaving the center almost concave, of pure white, with a small green eye . . . sumptuous and ravishing." The scent of Maiden's Blush reduces Sir Thomas to the rapturous ineffables of a trashy romance writer: her blooms are "intense, intoxicating, delicious . . . my senses have not yet found the means of conveying to my pen their qualities." Marie Louise, a rose raised at Malmaison in 1813, brings out the Humbert Humbert in him: "To lift up the leafy sprays and look steadily at the fully opened blooms is a revelation..." I was beginning to understand why rosarians tend to be men. Men, and then of course Vita Sackville-West, who could certainly work herself up writing about old roses: "Rich they were, rich as a fig broken open, soft as a ripened peach, freckled as an apricot, coral as pomegranate, bloomy as a bunch of grapes." Your opinion, Doctor Freud?

If the allure of old roses is in the frank sensuality of their blooms, then what are we to make of the development and eventual triumph of the modern hybrid tea? Maybe the Victorian middle class simply

*Schneider's Choice of 6 Roses*, late 1800s or early 1900s

couldn't deal with the rose's sexuality. Perhaps what really happened in 1867 was a monumental act of horticultural repression. By transforming the ideal of rose beauty from the fully opened bloom to the bud, the Victorians took a womanly flower and turned her into a virgin—a venerated beauty when poised on the verge of opening, but quickly fallen after that.

As for the prized new trait of continual bloom, that too can be seen as a form of sublimation. For the hybrid roses don't give more bloom, really, they just parcel their blooms out over a longer period; they save and reinvest. So instead of abandoning herself to one great climax of bloom, the rose now doles out her blossoms one by one, always holding back, forever on the verge, never quite . . . finishing. The idea of a flower that never finishes would have struck the Elizabethans as perverse; one of the things they loved most about the rose was that it held nothing back, the way it bloomed unreservedly and then was spent. But the Victorians bred this sexual rhythm out of the rose, subordinating it to the period's cult of virginity, as well as its new concepts of economy. From them we've inherited a girlish flower, pretty perhaps, but scrubbed to the point of scentlessness, no more alluring or sexually aware than a girl scout.

To look at a flower and think of sex—what exactly can this mean? Emerson wrote that "nature always wears the colors of the spirit," by which he meant that we don't see nature plain, only through a screen of human tropes. So in our eyes spring becomes youth, trees truths, and even the humble ant becomes a big-hearted soldier. And certainly when we look at roses and see aristocrats, old ladies and girl scouts, or symbols of love and purity, we are projecting human categories onto them, saddling them with the burden of our metaphors.

But is there any other way to look at nature? Thoreau thought there was. He plumbed Walden Pond in winter in order to relieve nature of precisely this human burden—to "recover the long lost bottom of Walden Pond" from the local legends that held it bottomless. Thoreau was confident he could distinguish between nature (the pond, which he determined had a depth of exactly one hundred and two feet) and culture (the stories people told about its bottomlessness); he strove to drive a wedge between the two once and for all—to see the pond with a mind of winter: unencumbered, as it really was. "Let us settle ourselves, and work and wedge our feet downward through the mud and slush of opinion, and prejudice, and tradition, and delusion, and appearance, that alluvion which covers the globe . . . till we come to a hard bottom and rocks in place, which we can call *reality*, and say, This is . . . " The transcendentalists looked to nature as a cure for culture, but before it can exert its "sanative influence," we have first to scrape off the crust of culture that has formed over it. This neat segregation of nature and culture gets complicated when you get to garden plants such as the rose, which perhaps begins to explain why Thoreau preferred swamps to gardens. For the rose not only wears the colors of our spirit, it *contains* them. Roses have been "cultivated" for so long, crossed and recrossed to reflect our ideals, that it is by now impossible to separate their nature from our culture. It is more than a conceit to suggest that Madame Hardy's elegance embodies something of the society that produced her, or that Graceland's slickness embodies something of ours. To a certain extent, the same holds true for all hybrid plants, but no other has received as much sustained attention from the hybridizer, that practitioner, in Shakespeare's words, of an "art (that) itself is nature." Thoreau could not have gotten what he wanted looking at a rose; the rose has been so heavily burdened with human "prejudice, and tradition, and delusion"—with human history—that by now there is no hard bottom to be found there. "The mud and slush of opinion" has been bred right into Dolly Parton; she's more a symptom of culture than a cure for it.

But if Dolly Parton suggests that our intercourse with nature will sometimes produce regrettable offspring, that doesn't necessarily mean we are better off with swamps. It is too late in the day—there are simply too many of us now—to follow Thoreau into the woods, to look to nature to somehow cure or undo culture. As important as it is to have swamps, today it is probably more important to learn how to mingle our art with nature in ways that culminate in a Madame Hardy rather than a Dolly Parton—in forms of human creation that satisfy culture without offending nature. The habit of bluntly opposing nature and culture has only gotten us into trouble, and we won't work ourselves free of this trouble until we have developed a more complicated and supple sense of how we fit into nature. I do not know what that sense might be, but I suspect that the rose, with its long, quirky history of give-and-take with man, can tutor it as well as, if not better than, Thoreau's unsullied swamp.

Even once we have recognized the falseness of the dichotomy between nature and culture, it is hard to break its hold on our minds and our language; look how often I fall back on its terms. Our alienation from nature runs deep. Yet even to speak in terms of a compromise between nature and culture is not quite right either, since it implies a distance between the two—implies that we are not part of nature. So many of our metaphors depend on this rift, on a too-easy sense of what is nature and what is "a color of the spirit." What we need is to confound our metaphors, and the rose can help us do this better than the swamp can.

That perhaps is what matters when we look at a rose blossom and think of sex. In my garden this summer, Maiden's Blush has flowered hugely, some of her blossoms flushed so deeply pink as to deserve the adjective *émue*. So what does it mean to look at these blossoms and think of sex? Am I thinking metaphorically? Well, yes and no. This flower, like all flowers, *is* a sexual organ. The uncultured bumblebee seems to find this bloom just as attractive as I do; he seems just as bowled over by its perfume. Yet I can't believe I gaze at the blossom in quite the same way he does. Its allure, for me, has to do with its resemblance to women—to "the thighs of an aroused nymph," about which I can assume he feels nothing. For this is a resemblance my species has bred, or selected, this rose to have. So is it imaginary? Merely a representation? (But what about the bee?! That's no representation he's pollinating.) Are we, finally, speaking of nature or culture when we speak of a rose (nature) that has been bred (culture) so that its blossoms (nature) make men imagine (culture) the sex of women (nature)?

It may be this sort of confusion that we need more of.

The Allure of Roses, hand-colored postcard, early 1900s

*Tulipe cultivée* (Variété)                                       *Tulipa culta* (Var.

P. J. Redouté. _ 142.                                                         Lang.

# The Tulip

## by Anna Pavord

*I*n this excerpt from her best-selling book *The Tulip: The Story of the Flower that Has Made Men Mad* (Bloomsbury, 1999), Anna Pavord delves into the remarkable history of this seemingly common spring flower. Pavord is also the author of *The Naming of Names: The Search for Order in the World of Plants* (Bloomsbury, 2005), *The New Kitchen Garden* (Dorling Kindersley, 1999), and *The Border Book* (Dorling Kindersley, 2000).

She writes for the London *Observer* and is the gardening correspondent for the *Independent.* Her articles have appeared in *Country Living* and *Country Life* magazines.

*Opposite: Tulipe cultiveé,* P.J. Redouté_142

*Above:* Tulips, *Photograph* © *Jane Booth*

157

The most interesting things in life often happen by accident. That is how I found myself one May sitting outside a taverna at Alíkampos in the western half of Crete, with no guide book, no decent map, but an excellent collection of wild-flower books. I spoke little Greek and the village elders solemnly ranged around the table—high leather boots, thorn walking sticks, moustaches luxuriant enough to hide a family of mice—spoke even less English. Small cups of coffee, tots of lethal, white, homemade brandy and dishes of salted marrow seeds piled up around us as the books were passed around from hand to hand, all open at the picture of the same flower. It was *Tulipa bakeri,* named after the man, George Percival Baker, who first exhibited it at a Royal Horticultural Society show in 1895.

It is not a particularly showy flower, compared with the wild, seductive, flamboyant tulips of the Crimea and Central Asia. The Cretan tulip is mauve-purple, with a pronounced and well-defined yellow blotch at its base. The backs of the petals are washed over with a faintly green flush, the overlay which gives so many tulips the texture of the finest, most luscious satin. But for some reason, I'd set my heart on finding it and Crete was its only known habitat. Intermittently, the Alíkampos elders set my flower books in front of me, opened at photographs of dragon arums, asphodels, and grape hyacinths. These, they indicated, they could show me by the hundred. But no one knew the tulip. More brandy was brought on to compensate for the disappointment.

Then, after a rapid exchange in Greek, one of the elders and a small boy beckoned me over to the hired car that I had parked nearby. I thought that they might need a lift, so we set off down the hairpin bends of the no-through road that leads to this hill-top village. Obeying violent hand signals from the old man, we bumped down a track off the road, parked, walked further down the hill and arrived suddenly at a small whitewashed building, no more than twelve feet by ten feet, standing by a spring.

The old man unlocked the door and, with a magician's flourish, threw it open. It was a church of course, though I didn't know that until I stepped inside and saw the grave, elongated faces of a whole lexicon of saints staring out with pitted eyes from wall and ceiling. Eighth century, said the man, tracing the figures with the end of a beeswax candle. Byzantine. He lit the candle and I peered slowly round at the ancient saints, the dark ochre colours of the paintings disappearing and then coming to light again as the candle flame bent and flickered. It was a weird moment: expecting tulips and finding frescoes instead.

Indirectly, the saints led to the tulip, for the small boy, left outside sitting on a rock, had hijacked a passer-by and showed *him* the picture of the flower that I was looking for. "Omalós," he said triumphantly as we emerged. "Omalós," he said again, pointing at the picture and then somewhere to the west, way over the horizon. The next day I drove myself to Omalós, along narrow roads lined with clouds of blue scabious and heads of wild oats and barley. The backdrop was gargantuan: stony mountain peaks with thick flanks of snow.

Omalós is a bleak town set high on a pancake plain, imprisoned between walls of mountain. The plain was nibbled bare by sheep. It was so quiet that you could hear the seed pods of the wild spurges popping in the heat. I quartered the ground like a blood hound, cheered at finding anemones in all colours, the wild forebears of the florist's 'De Caen'. It seemed likely that where there were anemones, there might also be tulips.

Without realising how much ground I had covered, I found after an hour or so that I was almost halfway up the mountain. The snow-line was clearly visible. I wanted to touch the snow and the track was easy. I calculated that it would take no more than a hour of climbing to get there. When I reached the snow, I found crocus on its melting edges. Even higher were flat, rock-hugging mats of an alpine anchusa, the flowers dazzling blue amongst the leaves. But no tulips.

At the top, I threw a snowball at an eagle before beginning a descent very much more rapid than the upward climb had been. Then, as I mooched back to the car, *Tulipa bakeri* suddenly sprang into view. I thought it was a mirage, but no. While I had been flailing up the "because-it's-there" route, they had been flowering in an area mercifully fenced off from grazing animals, on the old olive terraces of the

Omalós plain. They were growing in thin, poor grassland, their shiny leaves poking out from sheaves of anemones, with orchids thrown in for good measure, as well as the strange pale-green-and-black flowers of *Hermodactylus tuberosus.* I gazed at them in respectful—no, more than that—in reverent silence. I could find nothing suitable to say. This was the first time I had seen tulips growing in the wild. I knew how Galahad must have felt when he finally caught up with the Grail.

At this moment, I happily recognised an obsession that had been creeping up on me for some time. I suppose there must be one or two people in the world who choose not to like tulips, but such an aberration is scarcely credible. Who could resist *T. eichleri* from northern Iran, with its brilliant crimson-scarlet flowers, the petals nipping in slightly at the waist to finish in sharp needle points? The backs of the outer petals are washed over in greeny-buff, so in bud it looks very sober. Then it flings open its petals and reveals itself as the wildly sexy flower that it is. Who could not fall in love with the Cottage tulip 'Magier' as it opens its buds in May? The petals are a soft milky-white splashed with purple around the edges. As the flower ages, which it does gracefully and well (a worthwhile attribute) the whole thing darkens and purple leaches out from the edges through the entire surface of the petals. It is a mesmerising performance.

But as in any love affair, after the initial *coup de foudre* you want to learn more about the object of your passion. The tulip does not disappoint. Its background is full of more mysteries, dramas, dilemmas, disasters

*Tulipa Gesneriana* blooms in the wild in Europe during the months of May and June, *The Illustrated Dictionary of Gardening,* circa 1900

and triumphs than any besotted *aficionado* could reasonably expect. In the wild, it is an Eastern flower, growing along a corridor which stretches either side of the line of latitude 40 degrees north. The line extends from Ankara in Turkey eastwards through Jerevan and Baku to Turkmenistan, then on past Bukhara, Samarkand and Tashkent to the mountains of the PamirAlai, which, with neighbouring Tien Shan is the hotbed of the tulip family.

As far as Western Europe is concerned, the tulip's story began in Turkey, from where in the mid sixteenth century, European travellers brought back news of the brilliant and until then unknown *lils rouges*, so prized by the Turks. In fact they were not lilies at all but tulips; in April 1559, the Zurich physician and botanist Conrad Gesner saw the tulip flowering for the first time in the splendid garden made by Johannis

Two-Lips postcard, circa 1909

*Tulip Maja*, Manor House, Heslington, UK, *Photograph* © *Jerry Harpur*

Heinrich Herwart of Augsburg, Bavaria. He described its gleaming red petals and its sensuous scent in a book published two years later, the first known report of the flower growing in Western Europe. The tulip, wrote Gesner, had "sprung from a seed which had come from Constantinople or as others say from Cappadocia". From that flower and from its wild cousins, gathered over the next 300 years from the steppes of Siberia, from Afghanistan, Chitral, Beirut and the Marmaris peninsula, from Isfahan, the Crimea and the Caucasus, came the cultivars which have been grown in gardens ever since. More than 5,500 different tulips are listed in the *International Register* published regularly since 1929 by the Royal General Bulbgrowers' Association in the Netherlands.

Holland was the setting for one of the strangest episodes in the long, mesmerising story of the tulip. The 'Tulipomania' that raged in Holland between 1634 and 1637 has puzzled historians and economists ever since. How could it have ever happened that single bulbs of certain kinds of tulips could change hands for sums that would have secured a town house in the best quarter of Amsterdam? How was it possible that at the height of the tulip fever, a bulb of 'Admiral van Enkhuijsen' weighing 215 *azen,* could sell for 5,400 guilders, the equivalent of fifteen years' wages for the average Amsterdam bricklayer?

Certain facts are brought forward to support less certain theories. The setting-up of the Dutch East India Company in 1602 and Amsterdam's increasing importance as a port, marked the beginning of an era of great prosperity for the Dutch. Merchants became rich, and in their wake, lawyers, doctors, pharmacists and jewellers did, too. Adriaen Pauw, Lord of Heemstede, Keeper of the Great Seal of Holland and envoy of the States General to various foreign courts, was one of the directors of the new East India Company. His house, which was just outside Haarlem, stood in magnificent gardens where tulips grew clustered around a mirrored gazebo. The mirrors gave the illusion that the hundreds of blooms were thousands, for even Adriaen Pauw could not afford to plant thousands of tulips. For rich merchants, fountains, aviaries of rare birds, and temples in the Greek style were standard accoutrements of the garden. But the tulip was the ultimate status symbol, the definitive emblem of how much you were worth. In the 1980s, the City trader's Porsche performed the same function, though in a cruder way. Among the many rare tulips in Pauw's garden was the entire known stock of 'Semper Augustus', the most beautifully marked of all the red and white striped tulips of the early seventeenth century. By the 1640s, when tulipomania was officially over, there were thought to be only twelve bulbs of 'Semper Augustus' still in existence, priced at 1,200 guilders each. This was the equivalent of three times the average annual wage in mid seventeenth-century Holland, perhaps £80,000 in modern-day terms.

Tulips and bleeding hearts, Peggy and Tom Metcalf's garden, Deep River,
Connecticut, *Photograph* © *Jane Booth*

If you could not afford the flowers themselves, you commissioned an artist such as Ambrosius Bosschaert or Baithasar van der Ast to paint tulips for you. Even the grand master of Dutch flower painting, Jan van Huysum, could rarely command more than 5,000 guilders for a painting. But a single bulb of the tulip 'Admiral Liefkens' changed hands for 4,400 guilders at an auction in Alkmaar on 5 February 1637, while 'Admiral van Enkhuijsen' was even more expensive at 5,400 guilders. The last of the big spenders bid at this auction of tulip bulbs: ninety-nine lots which realised 90,000 guilders, perhaps as much as £6 million in today's money. Because the sale was held in February, while the bulbs were still in the ground, each was sold by its weight at planting time, the weights recorded in *azen*. Offsets carry the same characteristics as their parents. That is why they were valuable. They were the equivalent of the interest earned on the capital invested in the bulb. Tulip seed, by comparison, usually produces a wide number of variations on the theme of the parent bulb.

Selling tulip bulbs by weight seemed sensible but the system contained the germs of its own destruction. Once the concept of the *azen* had taken hold, these *azens* could be traded on their own account, without the bulbs actually changing hands at all. The *azens* took on a 'futures' life of their own and the tulip itself in Zbigniew Herbert's words, "grew pale, lost its colours and shapes, became an abstraction, a name, a symbol interchangeable with a certain amount of money". For this, tradesmen mortgaged their houses, weavers their looms. Many were bankrupted. Innkeepers flourished, for it was in the inns that most trading took place and the *drietje* or wine money was an integral part of each tulip deal.

In the end, there is no way to explain why tulip fever affected the solid, respectable burghers of Holland in such an aberrant way. They were possessed, obsessed by this flower with its intoxicating aura of the infidels who, as recently as 1529, had been battering at the gates of Vienna. And the flower itself had a unique trick which added dangerously to its other attractions. It could change colour, seemingly at will. A plain-coloured flower such as Councillor Herwart's red tulip, might emerge the following spring in a completely different guise, the petals feathered and flamed in intricate patterns of white and deep red. Seventeenth-century tulip lovers could not know that these 'breaks' were caused by a virus which was spread by aphids for the research that provided the answer to a mystery that had intrigued and ensnared tulip growers for centuries was only carried out in the late 1920s. Connoisseurs throughout Europe (and in the Ottoman Empire) had always rated "broken" flowers more highly than plain-coloured ones. For that reason, the broken flowers were the ones that commanded outrageous prices. But out of a batch of a hundred tulips only one or two would turn their coats each year and emerge the following season with highly desirable "feathered" or "flamed" flowers. As all the bulbs

Red and yellow tulips, *Photograph* © *Suzy Bales*

received exactly the same treatment, no grower could fathom the reasons for these differences. Each broken flower, each superbly complex pattern was as original as a fingerprint. The virus was the joker in the tulip bed. Since its cause was for so long not known, its effects could not be controlled. Fortunately, once a bulb had broken, it remained broken and the offsets produced by the bulb carried the same characteristics. But the virus had the effect of weakening the tulip, so offsets were not produced so freely and vigorously as might be the case with a virus-free bulb. Consequently, fine broken varieties such as 'Semper Augustus' were slow to increase, and that in turn increased their value.

The virus works by partly suppressing the laid-on colour of a tulip, its anthocyanin, leaving the underlying colour, always white or yellow, to show through. The contrasting red or purple of a broken tulip looks as though it has been painted on the petals with a fine camel-hair brush. Sometimes the feathered and flamed markings make symmetrical patterns and these were always highly prized by tulip fanciers. The contrasting colours of a broken tulip are always sharply defined, the effect quite distinct from the indeterminate flushes of different colours displayed on the backs of tulips such as 'Prinses Irene' or the rink and white species, *T. clusiana*, the Lady Tulip. The base of a broken tulip always remains pure white or yellow. The contrast between the purity of the base and the patterned petals was an important criterion of excellence among the florists who, from the middle of the seventeenth century, cultivated the tulip as one of six florists' flowers, shown in keenly contested competition.

Deeply intrigued by the process of breaking and spurred on, no doubt, by the thought of the vast sums of money to be netted from a good break, early growers noted the characteristic effects of the virus on the tulip—the mottled leaves, the smaller flower, the reduced vigour of the plant—without ever being in a position to relate effects to cause.

The very word "virus" was not understood in the modern sense until the 1880s. Only the advent of the electron microscope in the late 1920s gave researchers the necessary means to unravel its true nature. Aided just by the evidence of their own enquiring eyes, early growers had a thousand theories about the best way to bring about the magic break. Some charlatans sold miracle recipes for the purpose at a guinea a time. Some fools bought them. Pigeon dung was a favourite catalyst, as was plaster from old walls, and water that ran from dung hills. Some growers, taking their cue from contemporary alchemists, laid the desired colours in powdered paint on their tulip beds, expecting the colours somehow miraculously to transmute the flowers. It was no stranger than the alchemists' own attempts to turn base metal into gold. Indeed it was rather better, for while the alchemists consistently failed in their endeavours, it seemed that the tulip growers occasionally succeeded. They just did not know why.

Some old tulip growers tried cutting the bulbs of red-flowered tulips in half and binding them together with halves of bulbs of white-flowered tulips, hoping that a red and white striped tulip would result. It sounds crude, laughable even, but it was exactly by this means that the process of breaking was finally unravelled. It happened in 1928 when Dorothy Cayley (1874–1955), a mycologist at the John Innes Horticultural Institution in Merton, on the outskirts of London, grafted halves of tulip bulbs known to be 'broken' on to halves of the cochineal-red, Single Late tulip 'Bartigon' which were known to be unbroken. More than a quarter of the resulting flowers broke within the first year, a far higher proportion than in the control group. Earlier experiments on tulips at the John Innes Institute had been carried out by the botanist Dr E J Collins (1877–1939) who had suspected that aphids were the vectors, the carriers of the virus from bulb to bulb. He encouraged his pet aphids to gorge first on broken bulbs and then on bulbs that were presumed to be free of virus.

Unfortunately, his experiments were inconclusive because the so-called clean bulbs of the control group actually contained tulips that were already broken. But the deliberately infected bulbs did break over the next three years at twice the normal rate. The aphid in question, the most effective one at least, was *Myzus persicae*, the peach potato aphid, which flourishes in warm situations surrounded by an abundance of fruit trees. Fruit trees in abundance were an outstanding feature of seventeenth century gardens, and peach trees were particularly prevalent in the Eastern countries in which the tulip had its home. Although those early, observant gardeners realised that shifting their tulips into fresh soil often caused them to break more abundantly, none of them made the connection between the broken flowers, the fruit tree and its helpful, virus-inducing aphid.

The virus that affects the tulip is the only known instance of a plant disease which hugely increases the value of the infected plant. Since the turn of the century, however, when the single-coloured, mass-market Darwin tulips began to dominate the scene, breeders have done all they can to prevent breaking. The tulip, prized and cherished through more than 300 years as a jewel flower, refined and exquisite, revered for its individual intricacy, was redefined as brightly coloured wallpaper. Fortunately, it knows how to rebel. The joker still lurks in the tulip bed.

History is often interpreted through the laws and the wars that helped to shape it. The greater part of the book that follows is concerned with the history of a flower, but a flower that has carried more political, social, economic, religious, intellectual and cultural baggage than any other on earth. For centuries, it has invaded people's lives, demanding—and getting—attention both in the Ottoman Empire and in most of the countries of Europe. Under the Stuarts for instance, England witnessed two civil wars, a regicide, a republic, a restoration, and a revolution in breathless succession. But what was the gardener and staunch Royalist, Sir Thomas Hanmer (1612–1678) of Bettisfield in Flintshire doing during this time? With one hand he was levying 200 supporters of the King to help him defend his patch in north Wales. With the other he was sending tulips to John Lambert (1619–1683), one of Cromwell's generals. Lambert, like Hanmer, a besotted tulip fancier, lived at Wimbledon Manor, where he had a renowned garden. Hanmer sent him "a very great mother-root of Agate Hanmer", one of his best tulips, "grideline [a greyish-purple], deep scarlet and pure white, commonly well parted, striped, agated and excellently placed, abiding constant to the last, with the bottom and stamens blue."

Four Lovely Giant Darwin Tulips,
*Burpee's Bulbs for Fall Planting*, 1936

Throughout the cataclysmic events of the seventeenth century, the comings and goings of kings and protectors, the Gunpowder Plot, the Plague, the Great Fire of London, the tulip reigned, untoppled, on its flowery throne. It was the most sought after, most precious plant of the seventeenth century garden, the flower of the age, and like the age, intensely dramatic, prone to sudden change. This was not just in Britain. The tulip ruled all Europe, holding sway in the gardens of the Prince Bishops at Würzburg Bavaria, and at Nymphenburg Bavaria, the summer residence of the Electors; in the parterres at Schonbrunn, the Hapsburg palace in Vienna; in the Mirabelle Gardens originally built for Archbishop Dietrich outside the city walls of Salzburg; at Saint Cloud, Hauts-de-Seine in France where the Duc d'Orléans, brother of Louis XIV, employed the painter Nicolas Robert (1614–1685) to record his fabulous collection of tulips, variously described as *burinées, fouettées* and *pennachées*. Robert painted a striking, parti-coloured Parrot tulip of red, green and yellow; several red tulips, including the 'Jaspée de Haarlem', flared and streaked with yellow; elegant pale creamy-white tulips, touched at the edges of their petals with pink, and a deep-pink tulip, perhaps a fore-runner of the modern Lily-flowered types, pinched in very tightly at the waist and flaring out at the top, the petals tipped and streaked with green. Many of Gaston d'Orléans' treasures had been supplied by the Paris nurseryman, Pierre Morin, who had customers all over Europe.

From the late sixteenth century onwards, tulips, too, provided a map of the movements of the many people persecuted for their religious beliefs. Bulbs were valuable and they were eminently portable for refugee travellers. Like messages written in invisible ink, tulips emerged slowly in the new grounds that Flemish and French refugees were forced to seek in the wake of Philip II's Catholic crusades. In the second half of the sixteenth century, these Protestant Huguenots most probably brought the tulip into England from Flanders, for, long before

Five Giant Tulips, *Burpee's Bulbs for Fall Planting*, 1934

the Dutch cornered the market, Flanders was the most important centre of tulip breeding in Europe. Many of the immigrants were weavers and some settled in Norwich, at that stage the third most important city in Britain. Others, such as the Flemish botanist Matthias de l'Obel (1538–1616), settled round Lime Street in the City of London. A second wave of French Huguenots, including Maximilien François Misson, arrived in England in the 1680s, escaping persecution by Louis XIV, and furthered a massive explosion of tulip growing in England between 1680 and 1710. Huguenot refugees brought the tulip into Ireland too, where the Dublin Florists' Society was founded in 1746 by Colonel Chenevix, Captain Corneille and Captain Desbrisay, officers in the Huguenot regiments that had fought for Prince William of Orange at the Battle of the Boyne.

A thin, tenuous line marked the advance of the tulip to the New World, where it was unknown in the wild. The first Dutch colonies had been established in New Netherland by the Dutch West India Company in 1624 and Adriaen van der Donck, who had settled in New Amsterdam (Manhattan) in 1642, described the European flowers that bravely colonised the settlers' gardens. They were the flowers of Dutch still lives: crown imperials, snakeshead fritillaries, roses, carnations, and of course tulips. They flourished in Pennsylvania too, where in 1698, William Penn received a report of John Tateham's 'Great and Stately Palace its garden full of tulips. By 1760, Boston newspapers were advertising fifty

Darwin hybrid tulips *Tulipa 'Banja Luka'*, Castle Mainau, Germany,
*Photograph © Jerry Harpur*

different kinds of mixed tulip 'roots'. But the length of the journey between Europe and America created many difficulties. Thomas Hancock, an English settler, wrote thanking his nurseryman for the "plumb Tree and Tulip Roots you were pleased to make me a Present off, which are very acceptable to me." But he had changed his tune by the following year when, on 24 June 1737, he wrote that "The garden seeds and Flower seeds which you sold Mr. Wilks for me and Charged me £16 4s 2d Sterling were not worth one farthing. . . .The Tulip Roots you were pleased to make a present off to me are all Dead as well."

Tulips arrived in Holland, Michigan with a later wave of early Dutch immigrants, members of the Dutch Reformed Church, persecuted by King Willem I. Under their leader, the Rev. van Raalte, they quickly colonised the plains of Michigan, establishing, together with the many other Dutch settlements, such as the one at Pella, Iowa, a regular demand for European plants. The demand was bravely met by a new kind of tulip entrepreneur: the travelling salesman. The Dutchman, Hendrick van der Schoot, spent six months in 1849 travelling through the US taking orders for tulip bulbs. On 29 August he began the return journey to Holland, setting sail in the windjammer *Serapis.* "The ship rolls violently from side to side," he wrote in his diary. "High seas ahead—terrifying northwesterly winds—seas that reach to the heavens." He finally landed on 5 October 1849 at Hellevoetsluis, near Rotterdam, his order book intact.

While tulip bulbs were travelling from Europe to the States to satisfy the nostalgic longings of the first settlers, both English and Dutch, American plants were travelling in the opposite direction, often through the agency of John Bartram (1699–1777) who had established an important nursery and collecting point for American plants at Kingsessing, near Philadelphia. The new enthusiasm in England for American plants such as the red oak, the 'great laurel' (*Rhododendron maximum*), sugar maples and the beautiful *Stewartia malacodendron* was one of the reasons tulips dropped out of fashion in the gardens of the rich and famous. At this time too, there was a great change in gardening taste, which set the landscape style of Lancelot "Capability" Brown

(1716–1783) above the flower-filled parterres of the preceding age. The tulip in England was generally considered a French rather than a Dutch flower. As a result, it suffered in the rejection of all things French that followed the outbreak of the Seven Years' War in the middle of the eighteenth century. For all these reasons, the tulip lost its glamorous place in the most stylish gardens of England.

It was rescued from the dung heap by a completely different class of grower, men such as the Rev. William Wood (1745–1808), a Unitarian minister at the Mill Hill Chapel, Leeds, Tom Storer of Derby, railwayman and tulip maniac, who, lacking any garden, grew his tulips along Derbyshire's railway embankments, John Slater (c1799–1883) of Cheetham Hill, Manchester, who bred the supremely elegant feathered red and white tulip 'Julia Farnese' and Sam Barlow (1825–1893), whose life as apprentice, manager and finally proprietor of the Stakehill Bleach Works at Castleton could have provided the entire plot of an Arnold Bennett novel. They would have all described themselves as 'florists', using the word in its original, seventeenth-century sense; men who devoted themselves, singlemindedly, to the culture of a particular flower, who developed it by their own breeding to conform to a tightly laid-down set of rules, and who showed it in sometimes viciously contested competitions. Saddlers, glaziers, barbers and weavers were members of the Norwich Florists' Society in the 1750s. Shoemakers seemed to predominate in the Wakefield Tulip Society, founded in 1835.

The tulip, along with the auricula and the ranunculus was one of the six flowers cultivated as florists' flowers and in the careful, patient hands of the florists, the tulip reached its apogee. Hanmer and his like had bought their tulips at great expense, usually from European nurserymen. The florists, lacking the means to do that, grew their own tulips from seed, waiting seven years for a flowering bulb to develop from the initial sowing. Gradually, three clearly delineated groups of tulips emerged from the florists' breeding programmes: 'Bizarres' which showed red or dark purplish-brown markings on a yellow ground, 'Roses' which were white tulips feathered and flamed with pink or red and 'Bybloemens', white flowers marked with mauve, purple or black.

Tulips at Giverny, Normandy, France, *Photograph* © *Jerry Harpur*

The types had existed before, but the constraints of competitive showing put clearer markers between the groups and gave a little firm ground for judges to stand on. Frequent barbs in the *Midland Florist* and *Gossip from the Garden,* magazines founded specifically to cater to the needs of the florists, make it clear that judging was a dangerous pastime.

The uncompromising search for perfection in the English florists' tulip produced elegant beauties such as 'Miss Fanny Kemble', a Bybloemen with purple, almost black markings etched around the edges of the petals. The tulip had been raised in the 1820s by a Dulwich florist, William Clark (*c* 1763–1831), praised in his obituary as 'an honourable and upright man'. Purity was an obsession with tulip fanciers and both the base and the filaments of 'Miss Fanny Kemble' were extremely white and pure. It produced the famous 'stud' tulip 'Polyphemus' raised in 1826 by another southern grower, Lawrence of Hampton. 'Polly', as it was more familiarly called by the Lancashire growers who finally got their hands on it, was a Bizarre, highly rated for the pale lemon ground colour of the petals, against which the dark markings, feathers and flames, showed up dramatically.

Of the hundreds of tulip societies that once existed, only the Wakefield and North of England Tulip Society in Yorkshire now remains. Its dedicated members represent the last of the long line of amateur florists who have played such an important part in the development of the flower. In the petals of the exquisite, rare tulips still exhibited in competition each year by the Wakefield florists, runs the blood of flowers first grown by John Evelyn and John Rea in the middle of the seventeenth century.

English florists, though, were no less compromising than Turkish ones. In Turkey, tulips were such an obsession that an entire historical period, spanning the reign of Sultan Ahmed III (1703–1730) has been labelled the *Lale Devri*, the "Tulip Era." Three hundred years before the Royal Horticultural Society in England and the Dutch bulbgrowers in the Netherlands got together to prepare the first Classified List of tulip names, Turkish florists-in-chief were already setting up councils to judge new cultivars of tulips and give them official names. Whereas English florists favoured round, wide-petaled tulips, as close to half spheres as possible, the Turks only rated the dagger-shaped tulips made up of needle-pointed petals that feature so prominently in the decorative arts of the Ottoman period. *T. acuminata* was the species name given to this spidery, mad tulip, its tall, thin bud opening to creamy flowers, sometimes streaked and flecked with red. But although it is given species status, it is unknown in the wild, either in Turkey or elsewhere.

Fourteen different species of tulip can be found growing wild in Turkey, but probably only four of them, including the brilliant red *T. arimena* and *T. julia* are truly indigenous. The rest may have been introduced from similar habitats further east and became naturalised, particularly along old trade routes. Not long ago, I was in Eastern Turkey with my husband and two friends, looking for *T. armena* and *T. julia* in the areas around Erzerum, Hosap and Van, where the lake gleamed turquoise under mountains still covered in snow. It was May, and we ricocheted along roads and through snow-drifts that would have tested the toughest four-wheel-drive vehicle. We had a small, hired Renault saloon, but against all the odds, it survived, and carried us deep into the bare hills and rocky screes where pockets of bright red tulips grew among small geraniums and eremurus just coming up into flower.

*T. armena* or *T. julia?* It was a question we debated endlessly with almost every colony of red tulips we found. They seemed indifferent to the rules of nomenclature set down by taxonomists. On the road between Askale and Tercan, for instance, we came across an isolated group of tulips, with at least two dozen flowers in full bloom. Not one of them could be twinned with another. If you found two flowers that seemed the same, you would soon discover that their leaves were different. If sets of leaves seemed similar, then the flowers cocked a snook at you as they flaunted yellow feathering on their red petals, or showed that they could do without their black basal blotches altogether. We excavated one bulb and, before reburying it, established that it, at least, must have been *T. armena*, for it did not have much wool under its tunic. *T. julia* has a very woolly coat.

The loveliest colonies of tulips we found were in a valley above Tortum, north of Erzerum where groups of *T. armena* grew in little pockets between the limestone crags. We always found something intriguing there, sometimes a draba, sometimes an iris, once a wolf. That day, I was spread-eagled with my eyes closed, on a flat piece of rock in the sun. The *T. julia/T. armena* conundrum was rolling round my head like a riddle. I opened my eyes—who knows why—to find a wolf silhouetted against the sun. It sat upright, facing me on a neighbouring rock, its tail neatly curled around its front legs. Only inches from my eyes were the tulips, brilliant red blazes in the foreground. Behind them was the wolf, stark against the sky. When I sat up, it bolted away, disappearing into a low cave under a neighbouring rock crag. The conjunction of the two was as enigmatic in its way as the saints had been in Crete. As I lay on in the sun above Tortum, I thought still of these tulips, slashes of brilliant blood welling from the bare, brown, shale-strewn slopes of the mountain. Wolves were nothing to them. Saints were nothing to them. Millennia had passed by on this slope, while the tulip, mild as the wolf, slowly, joyously had evolved and regenerated itself. Even now, in their dark underground grottoes beneath the rocks, the tulips were plotting new feats, inventing themselves in ways that we could never dream of.

*Opposite:* Tulips, Mainau, Baden, Germany, *Photograph* © *Jerry Harpur*

# Daylilies

*by Sydney Eddison*

Sydney Eddison sings the praises of one of her favorite flowers, the daylily, in the following essay, which was first printed in her book *A Patchwork Garden: Unexpected Pleasures from a Country Garden*, published in 1992 by Henry Holt. Eddison teaches gardening at the New York Botanical Garden, and she is a regular contributor to *Fine Gardening* and *Horticulture* magazines. She is also the author of *Gardens to Go: Creating and Designing a Container Garden* (Bulfinch, 2005) and *The Gardener's Palette: Creating Color in the Garden* (McGraw-Hill, 2002).

*Opposite:* Bright Eyes daylily, Helene Ferrari's Hemerocalis Display Garden, Chester, Connecticut, *Photograph* © *Jane Booth*

*Above:* Ruffled Beauty, Helene Ferrari's Hemerocalis display garden, Chester, Connecticut, *Photograph* © *Jane Booth*

Having tried to copy an English perennial border without success, I was obliged to fumble along until I hit upon a way of gardening that fit the domestic landscape. It would please me more to think that one day I had suddenly come to my senses and said, "See here, you've got to stop trying to make an English garden and start thinking in terms of a garden that will suit this particular terrain and climate." But the revelation never took place, at least not just like that. What did happen was that in desperation—and because I didn't know what else to do with them—I planted twelve daylilies in the bank of fill that had been excavated for the garage. As soon as the first clump went into the ground, I knew I was on the right track.

A garden along the bank solved everything. East-facing and blending into the natural slope above the pool, it provided an almost perfect site for growing perennials—plenty of sun, good drainage, and with the woods rising behind and to the west, protection from the prevailing winds. It was also in full view of the terrace. The soil was terrible but there were things that could be done about that. I had finally found a permanent home for the perennial border—thanks to a dozen daylilies. I owe a lot to daylilies in one way or another. I love them because they are tough and easy to grow. They are survivors—and the most forgiving of perennials. Like most garden plants, they grow best in fertile soil that holds moisture—moisture is the vehicle for soluble nutrients; they prefer soil that isn't soggy either—if the air spaces in the soil are full of water, the roots can't absorb the oxygen the plants require. But they will grow in almost anything. Mine grew in fill—with the rather casual addition of some peat moss. For beginning gardeners, daylilies are ideal plants. Increasing in size and in the production of flowering stalks relatively quickly, they can soon be divided and spread around the garden. On the other hand, they will go on blooming prolifically for years without division; I am embarrassed to admit there are twenty-year-old clumps in my garden that have never been divided.

The flowers may only last a day but the plants are long-lived. Daylilies are often found around old houses and abandoned farm buildings. And roadside daylilies are the descendants of plants imported by the early settlers. In my own garden, there are masses of twenty-eight-year-old daylilies whose offspring are growing in gardens all over the neighborhood. I love some of the good old-fashioned cultivars, like 'Marionette' for their stamina, and expect them to be around when I'm long since dead and gone. It is a singularly comforting thought.

Most of all, of course, I love daylilies for their incredibly beautiful and abundant flowers. Their botanical name *Hemerocallis* comes from two Greek words— *hemera,* meaning "day" and *kallos,* "beauty." How could perfection be expected to last longer than a day? And their poignant underlying message of *Now! Do it now, enjoy it now, take it now!* is not lost on even the most literal-minded grower of this lovely plant. There is something to be said for having no past to regret or future to fear and for pouring everything into the moment.

Mapping Carolina daylily, Helene Ferrari's garden, Chester, Connecticut, *Photograph* © *Jane Booth*

I love the fact that daylilies are so easy to hybridize that far too many people get into the act and introduce far too many new cultivars. In 1987, there were 29,960 registered cultivars. I can't help feeling great affection for all these dear, crazy people of all ages and persuasions who become so enamored of these flowers that they can't stop breeding more and more of them. I applaud their wild dreams of a blue daylily—which I would personally hate—and a pure white—which I might like but feel, on the whole, I prefer the iridescent off-whites that glitter and gleam with hints of pink and mauve and peach. I particularly love these indescribable colors and the catalog descriptions of the indescribable. In one catalog, the cultivar 'Jim's Pick' has a base color in the morning hours of gold, which by afternoon is "smooth deep cream on which is blended the rose tones," which in turn blend into a "tangerine heart." To top it all off, "the raised ribs on each segment are orchid-pink and the edges of the petals burgundy or dusty rose." Whew!

Even in daylilies of a single color—a flower in which all the segments are one hue is called a "self"—the range is enormous. Wild daylilies display a range confined to shades of yellow and orange with timid excursions into the reddish tones. From this limited pallet, hybridizers have developed a spectrum that includes every ramification of yellow; reds and pinks—from the darkest to the palest; and royal purple and white, or so nearly white as makes no difference. Then there are the patterns: the shadings, bands, and water-marks around the eyezone; the edgings and even, perish the thought, polka dots. And the blends—two colors combined in a single flower. There is no end to the subtlety of the blends. And finally, back to the indescribable polychromes, such as 'Jim's Pick.'

Bless the hybridizers for their unrestrained creativity! Where once there was a single clarion form, there are now dozens of different shapes. Each flower is composed of an inner whorl of three petals and an outer trio of sepals—to be botanically correct, all six segments are called tepals. In wild daylilies, these segments are similar in design, relatively narrow and slightly flared—which gives the flower its classic trumpet shape. But modern cultivars come in all patterns and configurations. A side view can be described as flat, flaring, or recurved. From the front, the blossoms can look as round as buttons with wide overlapping segments or they can be star-shaped with narrower, outspread segments. So-called "spiders" have the narrowest and most widely spaced segments of all. And there are orchid-like shapes and

Miss Jessie daylily, Helene Ferrari's garden, *Photograph* © *Jane Booth*

tailored forms that are nearly triangular. The edges of the segments can be unadorned or blowsily ruffled, finely crimped or widely fluted. There are doubles with extra segments in all sorts of arrangements—from knots at the center of the flower to graduated hose-in-hose patterns in which sets of tepals are tucked one inside the other. It's hard to imagine where the ingenuity of the hybridizers will lead them next. But that's part of the charm of daylilies—and of their admirers. Nothing new under the sun? In the world of daylilies, there's always something new.

Daylilies were the first perennials I ever bought and it was love at first sight. My early composition books are filled with guilty admissions: "Have gone daylily-mad this year. I can't resist that half-price sale." Another year, "I've ordered a whole collection of pink daylilies. And I don't even know where to put them!" So it went over the years. And in time, an affair—at first, headlong and adolescent—

185

matured into an abiding love. The great range of flower sizes and heights alone make daylilies the most versatile of garden plants. These two elements give you so much to play with.

The flower sizes fall into three categories, which are of importance chiefly to breeders and to people interested in exhibiting at shows. According to the American Hemerocallis Society handbook, the flowers of a "miniature" must be under three inches in diameter. In fact, most miniatures nowadays are considerably smaller, which has been the aim of many breeders—the smaller, the better. The next size up is "small flowered" with blossoms from three to four and a half inches, and anything over four and a half inches is considered "large flowered"— which can mean anything up to nine inches in diameter. To a gardener, however, these categories haven't much meaning. An inch one way or another doesn't matter. It all depends on where and how you want to use the plants.

I must confess, I love all sizes—the great and the tiny and those in the middle. The huge ones—I have one called 'Yellow Pinwheel' with blossoms at least eight inches across—make a big, bold splash of color. Admittedly, the flower stalks—"scapes" to the cognoscente— are clumsy-looking and should be hidden by bushy, floriferous plants in the foreground. But at a distance, those magnificent flowers are a wonderful sight. In a large, informal country garden you need big plants. This was one of the things I discovered fairly early in my gardening career. A small plant surrounded by a great deal of space has very limited impact in the landscape—except en masse. However, in a more confined and civilized garden, smaller daylilies would be preferable. They have other advantages over the whopping big ones— the spent heads of miniatures and small flowered cultivars are much less noticeable and don't have to be slavishly removed, unless you are a perfectionist.

I love some of the immensely tall daylilies with small flowers. The scapes are so long and slender that they disappear against a green background and the flowers appear to float in space. Off in distant corners of the garden, I have clumps of a six-footer called 'Autumn

Watermelon Moon and Strawberry Candy daylily, Helene Ferrari's summer garden in Connecticut, *Photograph* © *Jane Booth*

Ruffled Beauty, Helene Ferrari's Hemerocalis display garden,
Chester, Connecticut, *Photograph* © *Jane Booth*

Minaret' which holds aloft clusters of starry yellow flowers. They are like a grace note in the landscape—just a touch of color, a small, welcome surprise. The tall ones are useful in a deep perennial border, too. Many plants that provide height also take up a substantial amount of lateral space but the tall daylilies require only a modest area. Flower scapes range from six-footers, like those of 'Autumn Minaret' down to wiry little stems only a few inches high. "Dwarf," a term which appears in daylily catalogs, applies to daylilies with scapes under twelve inches. The flower of a dwarf may be any size.

I don't think I have ever gotten rid of a perennial because its flowers were a disappointment. But any number of plants have left my garden via the back door because their foliage didn't pass muster. To be worthy of a permanent position in the garden, a perennial must have—at the very least—serviceable foliage which never goes through such an unattractive stage that it draws attention to itself. On a scale of one to ten, daylily foliage is below the very top—with hosta awarded a perfect ten—but well above the middle. Emerging from the ground as fresh yellow-green tufts in the spring, the long, folded leaves rise from the crown in pairs and arch over as they mature. Some have more upright foliage than others. The habit of growth and width of the leaves varies depending on the cultivar. Some of the miniatures have grassy leaves, while some of the strapping giants have great sheaves of upright foliage. The majority of the daylilies in my garden produce graceful fountains of leaves rising to different heights—again, depending on the cultivar.

For most of the season, daylily foliage adds to the attractiveness of the garden, supplying a pleasant green background for the flowers of earlier blooming plants, and those long, swishy leaves are a wonderful cover-up for the yellowing foliage of spring bulbs. For a brief spell immediately after flowering the outer leaves of a daylily clump go through their leaden hour—many of them turn partially brown. At this stage, they can be cut off without harming the plant. I sometimes cut down the worst offenders, but in a few weeks new leaves will appear anyway, and by fall the plants are perfectly respectable again.

It is worth mentioning here that daylilies have three types of foliage habit—deciduous or dormant, ever-green and semi-evergreen. Under-standing what these distinctions mean is far more important to gardeners than knowing that a miniature has a three-inch flower. Deciduous daylilies— as might be supposed—lose their leaves at the onset of winter and produce new ones in the spring. Evergreens—also, as one might imagine—retain their green leaves but—and here is the rub—in a cold climate, these can turn to mush and rot. The leaves of semi-evergreens behave in a manner halfway between the two—the part of the leaf closest to the crown stays green and the rest dies back.

Although foliage type cannot be used as a totally reliable guide to hardiness, as a rule of thumb, northern gardeners do best with dormant or deciduous daylilies and southerners do best with the evergreens. Semi-evergreens seem to have a very wide range of hardiness. And if you cover your daylily plants with six to eight inches of salt hay or shredded leaves in the fall, the chances are you can get away with growing all three types. I have been conservative in my choice of cultivars. I have only one evergreen about which I am quite passionate— 'Dwarf King,' a mini that has shocking-apricot flowers banded with a red eyezone. But this much loved and much admired plant is less vigorous than most of my other daylilies. The evergreen leaves die back to the crown in the winter and the plant doesn't increase in size as it should because half the clump rots every year. Not using a winter mulch—the garden is too big for that kind of extra care—I have usually stuck to dormant daylilies.

I can hardly bring myself to say a negative word about one of my all-time favorite plants but there is an observation I feel duty-bound to make. All daylilies are not created equal. Some hybridizers have concentrated so hard on flower forms and colors that they have neglected to put enough emphasis on the behavior of the plant—the appearance of the foliage, the strength of the stems, and the number of buds per stem. A daylily with only a few flower buds will be in bloom only a few days, whereas 'Sparks,' a wonderful militantly red-orange cultivar

Queens Navy, Helene Ferrari's garden, *Photograph* © *Jane Booth*

with small flowers, boasts as many as fifty buds to a stem and goes on blooming for weeks. 'Sunrise Serenade,' a cultivar with irresistible polychrome flowers of vast size and the most delectable hues—pink, lavender, and cream—cannot hold its own head up if two buds happen to open on the same stem on the same day. Naturally, catalogs neglect to mention these drawbacks.

In buying daylilies by mail, the beginner can't go too far wrong in ordering cultivars singled out to receive the Stout Medal. Awarded by the American Hemerocallis Society and named for Dr. Arlow Burdette Stout, the medal is reserved for the crème de la crème. Gardeners have Dr. Stout to thank for the breakthrough that dramatically increased the color range in hybrid daylilies and led to the development of the luscious reds and pinks we now take for granted. Purveyors of daylilies are not shy about calling attention to cultivars that have received the coveted Stout Medal. Another way to select good cultivars is to be guided by the popularity poll conducted each year among members of the American Hemerocallis Society. Catalogs regularly list award winners.

In addition to information about awards and each cultivar's bloom size, color, height, and type of foliage, catalogs also identify tetraploid daylilies by the abbreviation "Tet." Most daylilies are diploids with twenty-two chromosomes per cell. Tetraploids have double that number—44 chromosomes per cell—and as a result are larger and have more intensely colored flowers, stronger stalks, and lusher foliage. However, there is often a price to pay in loss of grace and elegance. This genetic manipulation is accomplished by the use of colchicine, an alkaloid derived from the autumn crocus (*Coichicum autumnale*), and the increase in chromosomes expands the horizons for breeders—which hardly seems necessary to me. Nevertheless, I have succumbed joyfully to tetraploid temptations such as the polychrome 'My Hope' and golden yellow 'Mary Todd.'

Daylily catalogs have always been my downfall. It takes a stronger character than mine to resist a notice like this: "May we help? We have put together several lists of daylilies that you may be looking for. We grow many TETS, DIPS, MINIS, DOUBLES, and SPIDERS, which we can't fit into our usual catalog each year. They range from the old and commonplace to the very new. Please let us know what interests you and send a self-addressed stamped business sized envelope." Well, of course, I will. I adore daylily lists and catalogs. I even love the fulsome, foolish, funny names. How about 'Blushing Angel' and 'Cherry Cheeks'; 'Gentle Sunbeam' and 'Heavenly Hope'; 'Eenie Weenie,' 'Cutie Pie,' 'Little You,' and 'Little Me Too.'

At breakfast, I pore over the names and descriptions and always find something that I can't live without. That is the problem with daylilies. After a while, your garden is full of them; the ones you already have are on the increase. You really haven't room for more but you can't help yourself, so you go ahead and order more. The new additions haven't a proper home, which leaves you three choices: discard something that you have had for years (heaven forfend!); cram the new ones into the overcrowded perennial border; or dig up more of the lawn and make another bed. I do a little of each. The design of the garden suffers but my thirst for daylilies is temporarily slaked.

In a big, rambling country garden there is nothing more right than masses of daylilies. Look at them along the roadside. What could possibly look more at home than a great bank of graceful, flowing leaves with hundreds and hundreds of slim, wiry stems—all leaning in the same direction and offering up a host of orange trumpet-shaped blossoms? Daylilies and a slope are made for each other, especially an east-facing slope like mine. Inclining gently toward the morning sun, each flower reveals the glowing color at the base of the corolla. The minute I saw the first scapes of 'Marionette' bending slightly toward the terrace and the pool and exposing the handsome dark red eyezone at the heart of the golden trumpets, I knew what to do next . . . if I added to the daylilies and extended the bed . . . if I brought up the other perennials from below and started working along the slope toward the evergreen garden at the far end . . . And that's just one more reason why I love daylilies.

# Mc GREGOR'S SPECIAL CATALOGUE

## BARGAIN SALE EDITION

### EVERYTHING AT REDUCED PRICES

**SPECIAL SALE OFFER**

The Wonderful Hardy
Monthly Blooming Climbing Roses
DR. W. VAN FLEET

stands at the very head of climbing roses. Th
flowers, when open, run four inches and over in di
meter, and are borne constantly from the time th
sun shines in the spring until late in the autumn.
Stems 12 to 18 inches long, making a fine rose fo
cutting. Grows vigorously and is immune from
mildew and other diseases.

Strong 1 yr. plants, postpaid — 14c  Stronger 2 yr. plants — 42c
Extra large 2 year plants — 69c (by Express only)
Extra heavy field grown plants — 93c
Largest Selected Field Grown Plants $1.42

The McGREGOR BROS. CO.,
SPRINGFIELD, OHIO, U.S.A.

WN ROM NATURE FOR GREGOR BROS. CO. RINGFIELD, OHIO. U.S.A.

# Cultivating Delight

*by Diane Ackerman*

Author Diane Ackerman is an acclaimed poet, essayist, and naturalist who masterfully combines her love of the natural world with her passion for the written word. Her published works include *A Natural History of the Senses* (Vintage, 1991), *The Rarest of the Rare* (Vintage, 1997), and *Cultivating Delight: A Natural History of My Garden* (Harper Collins, 2001), in which the following essay about her fondness for roses first appeared.

*Opposite:* Dr. W. Van Fleet Climber, The Bargain Sale
Edition of *McGregor's Special Catalogue*, 1911

Sitting at my desk one sultry morning, I'm distracted by beauty. Parked right in front of me is a teal vase containing a garden bouquet of twenty roses, a bright spectrum of colors: fuchsia, blue-red, talcy pink, peach, yellow-white (the Swan), purple-and-white stripe (Purple Tiger), orangey-cream tinged with pink (Abraham Darby), and a hot pink that verges on red (Leonardo da Vinci). They all have names, of course, such as Intrigue, Autumn Sunset, Lasting Peace, and Fame. Some open simply, others are densely ruffled. Some roses seem to be

McGregor's New Fancy Roses, offered in McGregor's 1911 catalog

tumbling from the squat round vase, tumbling yet stopped in midair. Others are braced by the lip of the vase, chins resting. Most are fanned out at different angles. But for the green foliage giving them a context and weave, they would seem to be floating clouds or a rose iceberg of different hues. The whole effect is beautiful enough to make one cry out, not in pain but in beauty. Wow! is as close as English lets us come,

but it falls short of the sensory stun of bold saturated colors and shapes sparklingly different and unexpected. Ralph Waldo Emerson wrote that there were times when nature made him glad to the brink of fear, and that captures it much better. Although everyone feels rivulets of wonder, and even bone-shaking awe, from time to time, not everyone is as comfortable expressing those feelings as freely as John Muir, Ralph

Pink Climbing Rose, Linda Wood's garden, Hope Valley, Rhode Island, *Photograph* © *Jane Booth*

Waldo Emerson, or Walt Whitman. I suppose what people fear is loss of objectivity. But life doesn't require you to choose between reason and awe, or between clearheaded analysis and a rapturous sense of wonder. A balanced life includes both. One of the fascinating paradoxes of being human is that we are inescapably physical beings who yearn for transcendence. One can be spiritual without believing in a supernatural being. Most often, the result is simply heightened emotion of a commonplace, gee-whiz sort. But someone like Lewis Thomas, for instance, had a real gift for conveying his sense of wonder in uniquely artful ways. Unfortunately, language really stumbles when emotions surge. So we don't have a precise vocabulary for complex feelings. Small wonder people resort to metaphors to express their raw joy, mysticism, and awe. There are moments when, as the poet Rilke puts it, "I would like to step out of my heart / and go walking beneath the enormous sky."

Anyway, the roses are blooming like a meteor shower, thicker and healthier than ever this year. Not just for me. My neighbors' gardens are luxuriant, too. Nodding peonies, unexpected blurts of dangling wisteria, thickets of oregano and Russian sage are taking over the neighborhood. But my roses are miracles. Carefree Wonder—pink with a talcy white back—is so bushy and bloom-laden it obscures a large window. The climbing red Blaze finally got the knack and is arching hugely on a trellis with a cascade of blooms. Red passionflowers and purple sweet peas climb the same trellises, but lower down. I've been able to make whole bouquets of one rose: eight Abraham Darbys or a dozen Dark Ladys. Most days I gather two to three dozen roses. Soon they'll rest some, and I'll mope until they flush again later in the summer. But at the moment it's a rose riot.

Choosing among flowers may be like choosing among children; each has its delights. But roses are the main flowers I bring indoors. My passion for roses borders on obsession. I have 120 rosebushes, and I feel that if I were to count them every day, *that* would be an obsession. I tell myself that at the moment it's just a hungry penchant allowed to run wild. Even though I have a splendid array of rosebushes, I keep buying more. I can't resist a healthy, heavily budded rose, and I rarely let the blooms stay on the bushes. The second they're ready to pick, I bring them indoors for arrangements. There are four dozen cut roses in the house as I write this, and more are coming into bloom each day, almost more than I can handle. I am besotted with roses—and I bought two more rosebushes in the middle of a bike ride this morning. My ride takes me past my addiction, two nurseries where my delicately petaled and perfumed drug is sold.

I'm not an expert rose person by a long shot, but when I go to garden shops, people often assume I'm an employee and ask for advice. I think it must be because they see me checking the roses so carefully.

Does this one have mildew? Does that one have black spot? How many buds are there? How much new growth? To my surprise, this year I seem to have acquired enough experience to be reasonably helpful. Most often they ask for fuss-free, surefire roses anyone can grow, and I suggest the pink Fairy, a hardy rose that blooms repeatedly until frost in my region, and which, for some reason, the deer don't eat. It has small flowers among the thorns and perhaps deer feel the blooms aren't worth the squirmish. I also suggest the

10c. worth of roses offer,
*McGregor Bros. Co.* catalog, 1912

Carefree roses—Carefree Beauty, Carefree Delight, Carefree Wonder—which handle diseases well and grow quickly into large luxuriant mounds of pink. Another good choice is the English tea rose Abraham Darby (named after a nineteenth-century British industrialist), whose scent is gorgeous, whose ambiguous color (a lightly stirred mix of apricot, pink, and yellow) is spectacular, which opens densely petaled, and blooms generously all season. If they like purple, Reine de Violette is just about the only purple rose I've found that's reliably hardy here. It has an unusual growing habit—very bushy with lots of leaves, among which sit many flattish, fluffy, grape juice-colored flowers. I think it looks more like a fruit bush than a rosebush. Blaze is the most popular red climbing rose for trellises, and, although it takes a few years to rise high and get solidly established, it produces fountains of red flowers. Old Blaze roses decorate many of the porches downtown, as if the homeowners have draped red flags from the roof. Othello is another good choice for a tea rose. It's sturdy, hardy, and can climb (one of mine is twelve feet tall). The flowers are huge, magenta, loaded with heavy scent. At the moment, my tall Othello, climbing the fence by the bay window, has fourteen large blossoms. People are often tempted by Don Juan, a dark red tea rose that's smolderingly beautiful and seductive. But I've found Don Juans to be delicate and easily shocked when transplanted. And you absolutely cannot pick one of the flowers until it's ready. Even then, it might not open fully if you pick it. Another red rose, the Squire, is a little more responsive, but also can be stubborn. Pick these roses when the petals begin loosening and they won't open indoors. I'm not sure why. They get water to drink in a vase; their stem is a straw for water on the plant. But they also need a chemical that signals them to flare. To be safe, with Don Juan and the Squire, I wait until the outer petals have pulled free and are admitting the air. If a traditional long-stemmed red rose is what they want, I suggest they try Chrysler Imperial or Mister Lincoln. Another favorite, which looks like it should be a real troublemaker but isn't, is the red-and-white-striped Scentimental, a rose with an unusually heavy scent and a festive look. But like most roses, these last five require some care. I could fill an entire chapter with favorite roses I find resilient and beautiful. I've bought several Canadian climbing roses, and I'm pleased by how well they survive harsh winters.

The more we know a thing, the more we appreciate its subtleties. I love my roses for their shades of difference, this one's sepals, that one's pink (say, Leonardo da Vinci's, only a hair's breadth more puce than Jean Piaget's). Such small shadings create individuals, perhaps with very different habits. Roses are *carpe diem* flowers—I'm never sure which ones will survive the winter. It's like adopting many children without knowing if they'll thrive. I appreciate them all the more for not knowing if this will be the only season I get to cherish their beautiful faces and fascinating ways.

Rose, where did you get your red? While taking my vitamins each morning, I sometimes pause at the lustrous oval gel of mixed carotenoids. If I took enough of them, I would turn orange; one can buy carotenoid pills that produce a suntan. Carotenoids give rose petals their red and fall leaves their shimmery scarlet oranges. I recently learned that roses have an enzyme that transforms carotenoids into the scent we associate with roses. This is just another example of nature's using one chemical in several ways. "How many things can you do with a pencil?" one might ask people, to encourage creative thinking. Evolution has been playing that game since the beginning of life. I would have said since the beginning of *time,* but of course life existed before time, a useful idea which is our own human creation, which we obsessively calibrate in terms our senses can fathom. Carl Linnaeus, the

World Renowned Cutflower Roses, *McGregor's Special Catalogue,* 1911

201

eighteenth-century botanist, even invented a floral clock. Noting that petals open and close at the same time each day (because they're synchronized to how much light they receive), he arranged flowers in sequence, using the movement of petals to tell time.

Variety is the pledge that life takes, and it doesn't apply only to chemicals but to behaviors as well, especially ones related to mating and child rearing. "Waste not, want not," an old adage goes. Redundant and wasteful as the brain can be with its cells, it also has evolved ways to use the same pathways for different tasks. Different trains travel on the same tracks. Not only brains use this strategy, flowers do too. Chemists have been diligently searching for the rose's aroma enzyme, because it's hard for perfumers to produce pure floral notes in a laboratory. Or for some flowers to produce them at all. When growers create the dazzling inbred garden plants we love, they often sacrifice aroma. Flowers forced to use their energy on color have little left for making scent, which means they don't attract as many pollinators (except humans). Thus my beautiful, tall, paint-splatter snapdragons are scentless. But a molecular biologist at Purdue just isolated the scent gene of snapdragons, and she plans on reinstalling the gene in descented flowers. Don't imagine this is an idealist's attempt to restore what was lost; she's also thinking about accentuating the scent of some plants. "If we can increase scent, for example, to apple trees," she explains, "the flowers will attract more pollinators or recruit new foragers. And that means better fruit quality."

I'm told fragrances sell more in summer than any other time of year, and that doesn't surprise me. All of nature is in bloom, oozing scent, lush with romance, and our instincts tell us to join the party.

When rose petals fall, the house looks littered with bright paint chips. They fall in slow motion and soft as rain. I like to lie on the couch with the back door open and two or three vases filled with roses on the coffee table beside me. The roses create a smell veil between me and the outside world. They bathe me in scent each time a light breeze touches them. In between breezes, they're still and my mind shifts to some other awareness. Then quietly, subtly, the roses begin mumbling scent once more.

Roses in a Country Garden, *Photographer © Richard Felber*

# Orchid Fever

*by Susan Orlean*

In "Orchid Fever," Susan Orlean describes in spellbinding detail the flower that has captured the hearts of collectors for hundreds of years. Orlean has written for the *New Yorker, Rolling Stone, Esquire,* and *Outside* magazines in addition to a number of books. *The Orchid Thief,* from which this essay was excerpted, was published in 1994 by Random House. The book was a *New York Times* bestseller and the basis for the movie *Adaptation,* starring Nicolas Cage and Meryl Streep.

*Opposite:* Vintage orchid illustration, from a private collection, used by permission

The Orchidaceae is a large, ancient family of perennial plants with one fertile stamen and a three-petaled flower. One petal is unlike the other two. In most orchid species this petal is enlarged into a pouch or lip and is the most conspicuous part of the flower. There are more than thirty thousand known orchid species, and there may be thousands more that haven't *yet* been discovered and maybe thousands that once lived on earth and are now extinct. Humans have created another hundred thousand hybrids by cross-fertilizing one species with another or by crossing different hybrids to one another in plant-breeding labs.

Orchids are considered the most highly evolved flowering plants on earth. They are unusual in form, uncommonly beautiful in color, often powerfully fragrant, intricate in structure, and different from any other family of plants. The reason for their unusualness has always been puzzled over. One guess is that orchids might have evolved in soil that was naturally irradiated by a meteor or mineral deposit, and that the radiation is what mutated them into thousands of amazing forms. Orchids have diverse and unflowerlike looks. One species looks just like a German shepherd dog with its tongue sticking out. One species looks like an onion. One looks like an octopus. One looks like a human nose. One looks like the kind of fancy shoes that a king might wear. One looks like Mickey Mouse. One looks like a monkey. One looks dead. One was described in the 1845 Botanical Registry as looking like "an old-fashioned head-dress peeping over one of those starched high collars such as ladies wore in the days of Queen Elizabeth; or through a horse-collar decorated with gaudy ribbons." There are species that look like butterflies, bats, ladies' handbags, bees, swarms of bees, female wasps, clamshells, roots, camel hooves, squirrels, nuns dressed in their wimples, and drunken old men. The genus *Dracula* is blackish-red and looks like a vampire bat. *Polyrrhiza lindenli,* the Fakahatchee's ghost orchid, looks like a ghost but has also been described as looking like a bandy-legged dancer, a white frog, and a fairy Many wild orchids in Florida have common names based on their looks: crooked-spur, brown, rigid, twisted, shiny-leafed, cow horn, lipped, snake, leafless beaked, rat tail, mule-ear, shadow witch, water spider, false water spider, ladies' tresses, and false ladies' tresses. In 1678 the botanist Jakob Breyne wrote: "The manifold shape of these flowers arouses our highest admiration. They take on the form of little birds, of lizards, of insects. They look like a man, like a woman, sometimes like an austere, sinister fighter, sometimes like a clown who excites our laughter. They represent the image of a lazy tortoise, a melancholy toad, an agile, ever-chattering monkey." Orchids have always been thought of as beautiful but strange. A wildflower guide published in 1917 called them "our queer freaks."

The smallest orchids are microscopic, and the biggest ones have masses of flowers as large as footballs. Botanists reported seeing a cow

The *Dendrobium suavissimum* orchid, illustrated by Paul de Longpré

Vintage orchid illustration, from a private collection,
used by permission

horn orchid in the Fakahatchee with normal-sized flowers and thirty-four pseudobulbs, which are the bulging tuber-shaped growths at the base of the plant where its energy is stored, each one over ten inches long. Some orchid flowers have petals as soft as powder, and other species have flowers as rigid and rubbery as inner tubes. Raymond Chandler wrote that orchids have the texture of human flesh. Orchids' colors are extravagant. They can be freckled or mottled or veiny or solid, from the nearly neon to spotless white. Most species are more than one color—they'll have ivory petals and a hot pink lip, maybe, or green petals with burgundy stripes, or yellow petals with olive speckles and a purple lip with a smear of red underneath. Some orchids have color combinations you wouldn't be caught dead wearing. Some look like the results of an accident involving paint. There are white orchids, but there is no such thing as a black orchid, even though people have been wanting a black orchid forever. It was black-orchid extract that Basil St. John, the comic-book character who was the boyfriend of comic-book character Brenda Starr, needed in order to control his rare and mysterious blood disease. I once asked Bob Fuchs, the owner of R. F. Orchids in Homestead, Florida, if he thought a black orchid would

The *Oncidium ampliatum majus* orchid, illustrated by Paul de Longpré

ever be discovered or be produced by hybridizing. "No. Never in real life," he said. "Only in *Brenda Starr*."

Many plants pollinate themselves, which guarantees that they will reproduce and keep their species alive. The disadvantage of self-pollination is that it recycles the same genetic material over and over, so self-pollinating species endure but don't evolve or improve themselves. Self-pollinated plants remain simple and common—weeds. Complex plants rely on cross-fertilization. Their pollen has to be spread from one plant to another, either by the wind or by birds or moths or bees. Cross-pollinating plants are usually complex in form. They have to be shaped so that their pollen is stored somewhere where it can be lifted by a passing breeze, or they have to be found attractive by lots of pollinating insects, or they must be so well suited and so appealing to one particular insect that they will be the only plant on which that insect ever feeds. Charles Darwin believed that living things produced by cross-fertilization always prevail over self-pollinated ones in the contest for existence because their offspring have new genetic mixtures and they then will have the evolutionary chance to adapt as the world around them changes. Most orchids never pollinate themselves, even when a plant's pollen is applied artificially to its fertile stigma. Some orchid species are actually poisoned to death if their pollen touches their stigma. There are other plants that don't pollinate themselves either, but no flower is more guarded against self- pollination than orchids.

The orchid family could have died out like dinosaurs if insects had chosen to feed on simpler plants and not on orchids. The orchids wouldn't have been pollinated, and without pollination they would never have grown seeds, while self-pollinating simple plants growing nearby would have seeded themselves constantly and spread like mad and taken up more and more space and light and water, and eventually orchids would have been pushed to the margins of evolution and disappeared. Instead, orchids have multiplied and diversified and become the biggest flowering plant family on earth because each orchid species has made itself irresistible. Many species look so much like their favorite insects that the insect mistakes them for kin, and when it lands on the flower to visit, pollen sticks to its body. When the insect repeats the mistake on another orchid, the pollen from the first flower gets deposited on the stigma of the second—in other words, the orchid gets fertilized because it is smarter than the bug. Another orchid species imitates the shape of something that a pollinating insect likes to kill. Botanists call this pseudoantagonism. The insect sees its enemy and attacks it—that is, it attacks the orchid—and in the process of this pointless fight the insect gets dusted with orchid pollen and spreads the pollen when it repeats the mistake. Other species look like the mate of their pollinator, so the bug tries to mate with one orchid and then another—pseudocopulation—and spreads pollen from flower to flower each hopeless time. Lady's slipper orchids have a special hinged lip that traps bees and forces them to pass through sticky threads of pollen as they struggle to escape through the back of the plant. Another orchid secretes nectar that attracts small insects. As the insects lick the nectar they are slowly lured into a narrowed tube inside the orchid until their heads are directly beneath the crest of the flower's rostellum. When the insects raise their heads the crest shoots out little darts of pollen that are instantly and firmly cemented to the insects' eyeballs but then fall off the moment the insects put their heads inside another orchid plant. Some orchids have straight-ahead good looks but have deceptive and seductive odors. There are orchids that smell like rotting meat, which insects happen to like. Another orchid smells like chocolate. Another smells like an angel food cake. Several mimic the scent of other flowers that are more popular with insects than they are. Some release perfume only at night to attract nocturnal moths.

No one knows whether orchids evolved to complement insects or whether the orchids evolved first, or whether somehow these two life forms evolved simultaneously, which might explain how two totally different living things came to depend on each other. The harmony between an orchid and its pollinator is so perfect that it is kind of eerie. Darwin loved studying orchids. In his writings he often described them as "my beloved Orchids" and was so certain that they were the pinnacle of evolutionary transformation that he once wrote that it would be "incredibly monstrous to look at an Orchid as having been created as we now see it." In 1877 he published a book called *The Various Contrivances By Which Orchids are Fertilised by Insects*. In one chapter he described a strange orchid he had found in Madagascar—an *Angraecum sesquipedale* with waxy white star-shaped flowers and "a green whip-like nectary of astonishing length." The nectary was almost twelve inches long and all of the nectar was in the bottom inch. Darwin hypothesized that there had to be an insect that could eat the unreachable nectar and at the same time fertilize the plant—otherwise the species couldn't exist. Such an insect would have to have a complementarily strange shape. He wrote: "In Madagascar there *must* be moths with proboscis capable of extension to a length of ten to twelve inches! This belief of mine has been ridiculed by some entomologists, but we now know from Fritz Muller that there is a sphinx-moth in South Brazil which has a proboscis of nearly sufficient length, for when dried it was between ten and eleven inches long. When not protruded the proboscis is coiled up into a spiral of at least twenty windings. . . some huge moth with a wonderfully long proboscis could drain the last drop of nectar. If such great moths were to become extinct in Madagascar, assuredly the *Angraecum* would become extinct." Darwin was very interested in how orchids released pollen. He experimented by poking them with needles, camel-hair brushes, bristles, pencils, and his fingers. He discovered that parts were so sensitive that they released pollen upon the slightest touch, but that "moderate degrees of violence" on the less sensitive parts had no effect, which he concluded meant that the orchid wouldn't release pollen haphazardly—it was smart enough to save it for only the most favorable encounters with bugs. He wrote: "Orchids appeared to have been modelled in the

*Miltonia bleuana* 'Morning Star',
from a vintage French botanical text

*Odontoglossum grande*, from a vintage French botanical text

wildest caprice, but this is no doubt due to our ignorance of their requirements and conditions of life. Why do Orchid have so many perfect contrivances for their fertilisation? I am sure that many other plants offer analogous adaptatior s of high perfection; but it seems that they are really more nitmerous and perfect with the Orchideae than with most other plants."

The schemes orchids use to attract a pollinator are elegant but low-percentage. Botanists recently studied one thousand wild orchids for fifteen years, and during that time only twenty-three plants were

driveways of fast-food restaurants, and in hot sand on a beach and in your hair on a windy day, and those will be swept away or stepped on or drowned without being felt or seen. But a few might drop somewhere tranquil and wet and warm, and some of those seeds might happen to lodge in a comfortable tree crotch or in a crack on a stone. If one of those seeds encounters a fungus that it can use for food, it will germinate and grow. Each time a hurricane hits Florida, botanists wonder what new orchids might have come in with it. At the moment, they are waiting to see what was blown in by Hurricane Andrew. They will know the answer around the seventh anniversary of the storm, when the seeds that landed will have sprouted and grown.

Nothing in science can account for the way people feel about orchids. Orchids seem to drive people crazy. Those who love them love them madly. Orchids arouse passion more than romance. They are the sexiest flowers on earth. The name "orchid" derives from the Latin *orchis,* which means testicle. This refers not only to the testicle-shaped tubers of the plant but to the fact that it was long believed that orchids sprang from the spilled semen of mating animals. The British Herbal Guide of 1653 advised that orchids be used with discretion. "They are hot and moist in operation, under the dominion of Venus, and provoke lust exceedingly." In Victorian England the orchid hobby grew so consuming that it was sometimes called "orchidelirium"; under its influence many seemingly normal people, once smitten with orchids, became less like normal people and more like John Laroche. Even now, there is something delirious in orchid collecting. Every orchid lover I met told me the same story—how one plant in the kitchen had led to a dozen, and then to a backyard greenhouse, and then, in some cases, to multiple greenhouses and collecting trips to Asia and Africa and an ever-expanding orchid budget and a desire for oddities so stingy in their rewards that only a serious collector could appreciate them—orchids like the *Stanhopea,* which blooms only once a year for at most one day. "The bug hits you," a collector from Guatemala explained to me. "You can join A.A. to quit drinking, but once you get into orchids you can't do anything to kick the habit." I didn't own any orchids before I went down to Florida, but Laroche always teased me and said that I'd never get through a year around orchid people without getting hooked. I didn't want to get hooked—I didn't have the room or the patience to have plants in my apartment, and I suppose I also didn't want Laroche to feel too smug about his predictive powers. In fact, nearly every orchid grower I talked to insisted on giving me a plant and I was so leery of getting attached that I immediately gave them all away.

Currently, the international trade in orchids is more than $10 billion a year, and some individual rare plants have sold for more than twenty-five thousand dollars. Thailand is the world's largest exporter of cut orchids, sending $30 million worth of corsages and bouquets around the world. Orchids can be expensive to buy and expensive to maintain. There are orchid baby-sitters and orchid doctors and orchid boarding-houses—nurseries that will kennel your plants when they're not in bloom and then notify you when they've developed a bud and are ready to take home to show off. One magazine recently reported that a customer of one orchid kennel in San Francisco had so many plants that he was paying two thousand dollars in monthly rent. There are dozens of orchid sites on the Internet. For a while I checked in on "Dr. Tanaka's Home-page"; Dr. Tanaka described himself as "A comrade who love Paph!" and also as "so bad-looking,

The *Oncidium Papilio Kramerianum* orchid, illustrated by Paul de Longpré

I can not show you my photo." Instead, his homepage had stories about new "splendid and/or marvelous Paphiopedilums in the Recent Orchid Show in JAPAN" and photographs of his greenhouse and his family, including one of his daughter, Paphiopedilum. "Junior high school, 1st year," he wrote under the picture of a smiling Miss Paphiopedilum Tanaka. "She is at a cheeky age. But I put her name to almost all selected clones of Paphs. First of all, I put 'Maid' and the next, 'Dreamy Maid', 'Maid's Happiness', etc." As for his wife, Kayoko, Dr. Tanaka wrote, "Her age is secret. She is worried about developing a middle aged spread as me. She never complain of my growing orchids, Paphiopedilums, and let me do as I like. . . . Before we have a daughter, I have put my wife's name to the all of selected clones of my Paphs. But after that, I have forgotten her name entirely."

I heard countless stories of powerful orchid devotion during the time I hung around with Laroche. I heard about a collector who had two greenhouses on top of his town house in Manhattan where he kept three thousand rare orchids; the greenhouses had automatic roof vents, gas heaters, an artificial cloud system, and breeze-simulating fans, and he, like many collectors, took vacations separately from his wife so one of them could always be home with the orchids. I heard about Michihiro Fukashima, the man who founded Japan Airlines, who said he found the business world too cruel, so he retired early, turned his assets over to his wife, severed all other ties to his family, and moved to Malaysia with his two thousand orchid plants. He had been married twice before and told a reporter that he felt "he had made his wives unhappy because of his orchid obsession." Charles Darrow, who invented the game Monopoly, retired with all his Monopoly money at the age of forty-six to devote himself to gathering and breeding wild orchids. A young Chinese collector, Hsu She-hua, recently described himself as a fanatic and said that even though he had been hauled into court four times for possessing wild orchids he considered it worthwhile.

Collecting can be a sort of love sickness. If you collect living things, you are pursuing something imperfectible, because even if you

manage to find and
possess the living
things you want,
there is no guarantee
they won't die or change.
A few years ago, thirty
thousand orchids belong-
ing to a man in Palm Beach
all died. He blamed methane fumes from a
nearby sewage station. He sued the county
and received a settlement, but began what his
family called "a downhill slide." He was
arrested for attacking his father, then for fir-
ing a sixteen-gauge shotgun into a neighbor's
house, then for carrying a concealed knife, pis-
tol, and shotgun. "It was the death of his

*Odontoglossum crispum*, var.
*Punctatum violaceum*, from a
vintage French botanical text

orchids," his son told a reporter. "That's where it all began." Beauty can
be painfully tantalizing, but orchids are not simply beautiful. Many are
strange-looking or bizarre, and all of them are ugly when they aren't
flowering. They are ancient, intricate living things that have adapted to
every environment on earth. They have outlived dinosaurs; they might
outlive human beings. They can be hybridized, mutated, crossbred, and
cloned. They are at once architectural and fanciful and tough and
dainty, a jewel of a flower on a haystack of a plant. The botanical com-
plexity of orchids and their mutability makes them perhaps the most
compelling and maddening of all collectible living things. There are
thousands and thousands of orchid species. New orchids are being
created in laboratories or being discovered every day, and others are
nearly unfindable because they exist in tiny numbers in remote places.
In a sense, then, the number of orchid species on the planet is
uncountable because it is constantly changing. To desire orchids is to
have a desire that will never be, can never be, fully requited. A collector who wants one of every orchid species on earth will certainly die
before even coming close.

Though my story was too personal to share
with most people, the garden seemed to understand;
it silently soaked up my sorrow and grief.
It gave me solace. I may have been on my hands
and knees in the dirt, but I was making progress,
physically and spiritually.

—Pat Bullard, *Fine Gardening*, April 1997

*Chapter 6*

# On the Mend in the Garden

**Opposite:** Campo de' Fiori, Sheffield, Massachusetts, designed by Barbara
Bockbrader, *Photograph* © *Jane Booth*

**Above:** Moody morning in a New England Garden, *Photograph* © *Richard W. Brown*

**dorless Marigold-Crown of Gold**
l-America Gold Medal Winner 1937. First
own Marigold with odorless foliage,
wer petals curled and quilled of golden
ange, sweet scented on long stems, early
wering, plants about 2 ft. tall.
**75 seeds 5¢; 200 seeds 10¢.**

**Verbena—Floradale Beauty**
Extremely large flowers; the giant florets
are usually over an inch across forming very
large flower heads, which vary in color from
rose-red to bright rose-pink. Easy to grow and
very showy in the flower garden.
**50 seeds 10¢; 80 seeds 15¢.**

**New Salvia—Blaze of Fire**
outstanding Novelty—plants dwarf and
shy with many flower spikes blooming
to 12 days earlier than any other dwarf
via and much brighter in color. Ideal
bedding or borders.
**30 seeds 10¢; 50 seeds 15¢.**

**iant Winter-Flowering Pansies**
e of the greatest horticultural introduc-
s in years. Plants grow 2 to 3 ft. high
h several strong upright stems bearing
ny blooms on flower stems 8 to 12 in.
. Grow inside in pots. Culture on pkts.
s scarce. **6 seeds 10¢; 12 seeds 15¢.**

**Giant ASTER NOVELTY** $100. for Name

Test Packet (20 seeds) included Free with every 1939 Order. Any person aft
growing it is eligible to enter $100. naming contest. *Rules & instructions on pk*

This Aster Novelty is being sent out to see if it comes true in all sections. O
Trials produced **Giant Flowers** in several shades of **Lavender** with White, strip
on edges of petals. *It is much more beautiful than Artist's painting of Flowe*

# B. MILLS Seed Grower, ROSE HILL, N.

# A Garden Cultivates Pure Joy

*by Dayle Allen Shockley*

In the following essay, Dayle Shockley finds respite in the garden during a particularly rough time in her life. Shockley is an author and a writing instructor in Houston. Since 1987 her work has appeared in dozens of publications. "A Garden Cultivates Pure Joy" first appeared in the *Dallas Morning News* on Tuesday, April 4, 2006. She can be reached at dayle@dayleshockley.com, or from her website at www.dayleshockley.com.

*Opposite:* Giant Winter-Flowering Pansies, Blaze of Fire Salvia, and Floradale Beauty Verbena, *Mills Seeds* catalog, 1939

I've been playing in the dirt since I was a toddler making mud pies—and occasionally eating them—but my first real experience with gardening occurred in the summer of 1989 when my husband and I became homeowners. I loved everything about the house—except the front yard. It resembled a jungle. Overrun with weeds and endless patches of crabgrass and dandelions, the worst part was there were no flower beds.

I had always dreamed of a yard filled with flowers, but I knew nothing about gardening, and with a toddler to chase all day, I wondered if there would ever be time for such things.

As the months unfolded, I found myself consumed with the tasks involved in settling into a new home. I forgot all about flower beds until one spring morning when I walked to the front door and saw Amy, my neighbor across the street, digging in the dirt around a couple of rose bushes. She appeared to be working hard, but I noticed a pleasant look on her face.

Suddenly, she looked up, saw me, and waved in my direction. So inviting was her wave that I scooped up my daughter and headed to the

Vintage seed packets, Dianthus, Aster, and Canterbury Bells,
Tregunno Seeds Limited

garage. Emerging with a rusty trowel, an old shovel, and heart full of hope, I marched relentlessly down the driveway. I would have a flower garden if it killed me.

And it nearly did. My back throbbed, my hands ached, my legs cramped, but by sundown, a small patch of ground had been cleared. I'd never been more exhausted and exhilarated all at once. I walked over and sat a spell with Amy. She offered an encouraging hug and enough gardening tips to fill a book.

The next few days were spent preparing the soil and making mental notes about the sun's path across the flower bed. Finally, it was time for the real fun to begin.

I drove to the local nursery and was immediately drawn to the impatiens. Delicate and dressed in soft colors, they quickly had me under their spell—not to mention they'd be perfect for my half-shaded flower bed. Satisfied with my choice, I loaded down a wagon with three flats of mixed colors, then picked up some liriope for the sunnier spots. Just as I was about to leave, something caught my eye.

Leaning against the gate was an old whiskey barrel, appearing a bit lonely and down-and-out. Suddenly—a vision!

"How much for the barrel?" I asked the boy at the register.

He studied it a moment, then said, "You want that barrel? Just take it."

So I did.

Back at the house, I lifted the young plants from their cramped quarters and began gently placing them in the damp earth. As they settled into the ground, my hopes settled right along beside them.

Now it was time to see what kind of magic I could work with the worn-out barrel. Placing it on its side, I pressed it firmly down into the soil, just behind the largest group of impatiens and—just like that—my vision sprang to life.

From where I stood, it appeared as if impatiens were spilling out of the barrel's mouth in a cascade of colors. Perfect! The only thing left was to water and mulch and scatter a few smooth stones around the edge of the bed.

As I took a step back, the transformation blew me away. Where once had been nothing but a sad collection of unruly weeds growing along the front of my home, now sat clusters of vibrant plants—some tumbling out of a whiskey barrel, mind you—all nodding at me as if to say, "We like it here."

The next morning, I rushed outside to see how the impatiens had survived their first night together. Rounding the corner, I caught my breath in sheer glee. The sight of their delicate faces, dappled with April's sun, made me wonder if I'd ever seen anything so beautiful. Quite frankly, I almost wept.

Each day that followed found me investing time and energy in the realization of a flower garden. It wasn't a big garden, nor that fancy, but

Garden walk with lambs ear, liatris, meadow sage, and astilbe,
*Photograph © Richard Felber*

it was mine. I gladly fed and watered. I pruned and weeded. And I was not disappointed. The more I offered the seedlings, the more they yielded.

One afternoon, I was stunned when a member of the homeowners association board brought over a sign that read Yard of the Month. I felt like a proud mother showing off her dressed-up children, but the truth is, it didn't matter to me whether anybody else noticed or not; I loved my garden for what it gave to me, alone. Many evenings I pulled up in the driveway exhausted from a long day at the office, but the minute I stepped out of the car and caught sight of the myriad shades and textures gathered in front of my house, I couldn't help smiling. Without making a sound, the garden had refreshed my weary spirit.

Seventeen years later, I'm as passionate about gardening as I ever was. Even though my body still punishes me for my enthusiasm, I feel more alive in my garden than anywhere in the world.

When you take a scrap of ground, turn it with your own hands, place tender sprouts into it and nurture them to maturity, you reap a joy that is hard to describe. It's a lot like raising a child. You're contributing to the cycle of life, connected to something much bigger than yourself. And when you walk outside and see an orderly assortment of colors and textures where chaos once reigned, it leaves you breathless. You realize that no matter how much you give to your garden, what it gives in return is so much more.

This was never so apparent to me as it was in the spring of 1999. The previous year had left me devastated by events out of my control. Getting out of bed each morning proved a struggle. A spring garden was out of the question.

But one weekend my mother came to visit and noticed the gloomy spot where flowers generally bloomed.

"You're not planting any flowers this year?" she asked one evening.

"I'm just not up to it, Mother," I said. "There's always next year."

A few days later, she wrote, "I'm sending you money for flowers. I want to do this, so let me."

I knew better than to try and stop her. Besides, maybe a little gardening would cheer me up.

Watering cans, Glen Dona's garden in Chester, Connecticut, *Photograph* © *Jane Booth*

With Mother's generous offering, I picked out an assortment of begonias—pink, red, white—and placed them in the ground. A few large impressive rocks for accents, and a Boston fern for a hanging stand in the deep-shaded area, completed the space. It wasn't much, but it would have to do.

In the weeks that followed, I spent time outside doing all the things that make a garden grow. And a curious thing happened. As I piled up spent blooms and pesky weeds on the ground beside me, my heart felt noticeably lighter. Liberated. Alive. Somewhere inside of me, a channel seemed to open up. Before long, I began talking to God as I worked.

Later I would write about it in my journal, about how spending time in my tiny garden helped me heal, emotionally. "I found strength in my garden today," I wrote one evening. "God was there."

Someone asked me once what I had learned from gardening.

Where do I begin?

For starters, there's patience. The heart of the gardener must be ruled by patience. You plant. You water. You weed. You feed. And you wait. You wait for growth. You wait for rain. And sometimes you wait for the rain to stop.

I've learned the importance of persevering. To expect that every year will produce a bountiful garden is a mind-set destined for disappointment. Some years bring an onslaught of storms, while others offer unrelenting heat and drought. But gardeners are eternal optimists. They understand that the nature of a garden is to persevere, to rise triumphantly above obstacles, to defy anything that would hold it down. It is this that keeps them going back, year after year.

Then there's the matter of those tenacious weeds. Even they offer a valuable lesson. Nipping things in the bud saves you precious time and effort down the road, and, as I discovered for myself, the simple motion of weeding can have remarkable effects on a weary spirit.

And finally, there is faith. Faith that you will walk past the window in the early evening and catch a glimpse of pastel blossoms dancing in the fading light, like so many fair-haired children. Faith that come sunrise they will be there still, to charm you once again.

No matter how I may be feeling when I reach for my trowel and spade—angry, despondent, frightened—time spent in the garden nourishes my soul and lifts my spirits. I've discovered that I cannot be truly sad and garden at the same time. But how could I be?

The very act of gardening is an exercise in hope. It is a lesson to the human spirit about turning nothing into something spectacular.

Lady Bird Johnson had a favorite saying: "Where flowers bloom, so does hope."

I couldn't agree more.

*Pois de senteur*, P.J. Redouté_70

# In Grammy's Garden

*by Lela Nargi*

Author Lela Nargi watches as her mother, who is caring for the ailing "Grammy" one summer, tends to Grammy's beloved vegetable garden with care, yet allows the weeds free rein. Nargi's writings on food and travel have been published in numerous magazines. She is the author of *All U Can Eat: A Cookbook for Beginners* (Princeton Review, 1996) and *Around the Table: Women on Food, Cooking, Nourishment, Love . . . and the Mothers Who Dished it Up for Them* (Tarcher, 2005).

*Opposite:* Dilly beans, fresh herbs, and tomatoes, garden of Bill Whitney, Truro, Massachusetts, *Photograph* © *Jane Booth*

The beets buried in Grammy's garden push tufts of dark greenery up through the surface of the dry July earth. Not only the beets but all the garden's crops are flourishing. Beds of arugula bear new leaf one day after another. The sunflowers burst and are still lively. Tomato vines bow under still-green but ever-plumping fruit. Melon and squash plants fire off flowers faster than anyone could count. The flowers are paler than daylilies—more peaches-and-cream than tangerine—and daintily, misleadingly unhurried. One day they show no interest in bearing fruit, the next morning you find a zucchini the size of a toy boat docked under an awning of leaves. In this extravagance of growth, every plant in the garden seems bent on reaching sooner demise.

This year, for the first time, Grammy has played no part in the crops' success, didn't sow or tend a single one. My mother inherited the task—happily, let me add, unlike certain other chores she accepted this irregular summer. It's possible that my mother acted autonomously in the garden's planting: scattered whatever seeds she found left over from last season in baskets on the old house's breezeway, or picked up a few packets of her own favorites at the nursery across the Connecticut

Marigolds, Nasturtium, and Chrysanthemum vintage seed packets

River, across the state line, in Bellows Falls. More likely, she followed militant instructions wheezed to her from Grammy in her cigarette smoke–clogged room. For reasons that have only begun to push upon my consciousness, it occurs to me that this particular detail—who decided what, all those months ago—has become irrelevant.

Grammy's garden is a large square plot. It's the final punctuation for an exclamation point of lawn that unfurls a few hundred feet off the back of the listing white Colonial Grammy called home for thirty-eight years. The lawn is flanked by foxglove and delphinium. In a corner at one end stands a red plaster Chinese statue, which Grammy, confusing stereotypes, refers to as Cho-Cho San. "San" stands between a short stone bench and a white pine ringed by lavender hostas. Behind this under-appreciated trio—no one I know of has ever rested for a spell on the bench, or admired San's chiseled features, or remarked on the flowers' faint sweet scent—runs a weathered wood fence, the same kind of hasty, post-and-lintel construction you find around gardens all across New England. If you weren't otherwise informed, you might think the fence marked the final frontier of Grammy's property. This is an easy mistake to make. Grammy's brand of order requires that the grass be mown nearly bald and the flowers kept sequestered in their lawn-side beds (a hired landscaper carries out both directives twice monthly, even now). But just over the fence, in Grammy's garden, chaos reigns.

This summer, my mother has coaxed a bounty of fruits and vegetables from the garden. And yet, for reasons she has chosen not to tell, she has also abandoned its weeding. Above and between the beets the crab grass thrives. It is undulant and thick, arching like a series of low tunnels. The soil around the romaine is clogged with clover-clone oxalis—whole networks of branches spotted with warm, yellow flowers. Chickweed has woven its threads through the tomato vines, stitching the vines to each other, and to itself, and to the ground that bore it, forming a tapestry ornamented with its tiny petioles. There are ferns in with the blackberry bushes, and sandwort stalking the string beans.

I think it's fair to say that the weeds are having their day.

Grammy would rage to discover her garden's disorder, and really, who could blame her? Thirty-eight years of plotting and planning; thirty-eight seasons of potato-bed inspections and threats to runted pea shoots; thirty-eight summers training vines to climb, and snapping back the fingers of wayward creeping tarragon, and ensuring that every plant—from carrots to peppers to broccoli—remains rigidly in line. And for what? To have dandelions shimmying under the gate to sidle up to the onions, and wild cress dancing across once clear-cut footpaths. You can be sure such a free-for-all garden fiesta would not suit Grammy's affinity for a geometry of alternating stripes of leaf and loam. Grammy is the sort of gardener who would find rapture in the farms of the flatlands which, seen from the air, present whole

Cabbage, tomatoes, herbs, and onions, garden of Robert Dash,
*Photograph © Suzy Bales*

hectares of corn and wheat and barley as repeating squares on a panoramic checkerboard.

Luckily, Grammy will never get wind of the garden's disarray. A few months ago, she abandoned home and moved into an apartment at the assisted-living complex. A 66-pound queen bolstered in her bed by a dozen pillows, Grammy rules a court of one—my mother—dispatching her in the few hours she visits every day to buy cigarettes and vodka, change the canister in her oxygen tank, lodge a barrage of complaints against the on-staff nurses, dose her with pills. This leaves little time for garden reports. Even the occasional garden drop-in is out of the question. This is because Grammy, languishing in the throes of late-stage lung cancer, cannot walk, can barely breathe, and drifts in and out—mostly out—of consciousness like someone who has been lured already by the shadow world behind her eyelids.

Still (How? Why?), as far as Grammy is concerned, the garden remains well within her sway. "Plant three *dark*-yellow marigolds between the rows of tomatoes and one *light*-yellow marigold at the end of each row of beans." This is typical of the specificity of commands Grammy continues to sputter to my mother from her bed. Although Grammy has no way of discovering if her demands are met, my mother always complies. This is because Grammy possesses a great talent for nurturing plant life. An enormous avocado tree she started from a pit in 1962 snakes from the foyer, up the banister in the old house to the second floor. Grammy's potted Christmas cactuses flower twice a year without fail. Her "culinary" specialties—dilly beans, dry-roasted tomatoes, pickled cauliflower—were born of annual overabundance. Plants obey Grammy and she lavishes them in return. The only growing things Grammy can't abide are weeds, probably because they have no need of her particularized ministrations. Grammy considers weeds so contemptible she could not imagine that anyone would grant them license to exist. And so it has never occurred to her that my mother, of all people, would think to give them refuge.

For one entire growing season, my mother has followed Grammy's gardening instructions to the letter. As these instructions have never

Gardener Deb Paulson of Chester, Connecticut,
with just-picked green beans, *Photograph © Jane Booth*

touched upon the matter of weeds, my mother has let the weeds be. My mother is neither an idiot nor an inexperienced gardener. If she hadn't been called upon this summer to care for an ailing Grammy, she would be tending her own garden in North Carolina, which is neat, weedless, and cyclically ripe with asparagus, chamomile, and strawberries. Nor is my mother negligent or spiteful; she has simply stumbled on a loophole in Grammy's details. Like magic, certain details have become generalities, their strictures softened to whimsy. To Grammy, who is unconscious of any shift, the details are the same as ever. The garden remains an ordered kingdom in her mind, and she is its exiled sovereign. But under my mother's lenient guardianship, the garden has acquired a peculiar life of its own.

The garden is cloaked, now, in the mesmeric, peaceful air of a cemetery, the sort of cemetery you might happen upon when you tread a country lane and pick through brambles to enter. In such a place, ancient headstones are plain and thin and crookedly set; ivy-swaddled shade trees refresh on blistering days; wildflowers are thick and irrepressible, so lush and spirited that, surrounded by the irrefutable absoluteness of death, your thoughts never stray to morbidity. Grammy's garden smacks of my mother's own sanctuary.

Scabbed oaks fortress the garden's perimeter, permitting sun to fall in for a few hours at midday and hiding all the outside world from view. Moss softens three good sitting stones just to the left of the gate. The crab grass stirs with a rustle and a hush. The oxalis, for its giddy expanse, is delicate in its way—pale and diaphanous, a loose cloud lying low, like night fog. The ferns are a catchall for berries, cupping juicy fallen ripe ones in their fronds. Reaching your hand in to pluck a nibble, you find that the ground there, in fern shade, is as cool as frost.

To one side of the central path, a plot that was neither tilled nor seeded this year sways with incidental plumage: willow asters, holding up their heads of hair-thin petals; blue-speckled blooms of Virginia dayflower; miniature chrysanthemums, not wild but also not invited. On the other side of the path, intermittent with the beans and tomatoes and squashes, larkspurs gust from stalks like tiny wind socks. Celadine dangles bean-like buds, which open into blossoms the color of butter. All through the garden the ground-cherry runs amok; beyond a hedge of thistle, on the far side of a flock of daisies, dangle its bright yellow bells. Closer, you notice that the pods that sprung them are slightly pointed, like hairless tomatillos, and so translucent that you can make out the berries coddled still inside. Grammy's garden, even as its weeds and crops hurry toward death, breathes with unexpected life and the promise of more to come.

In one notch of garden, adding a hint of intrigue to a thatch of low carrot tops, gangles one unique and inexplicable specimen. Its stem is the width of bamboo, its leaves are frizzed like kale. It holds aloft, 5 feet from the ground, a solitary bud as big as an egg. The bud is ballerina pink and so tightly clenched you couldn't pierce it with a pin. My mother says it has held its grip like this for three weeks or more, never so much as loosening a petal. She scrutinizes it often, hoping for an ounce of give and also, that it will open to a flower before it's time for her to leave for home. My mother is at a loss to say what this bud could be, and she would not ask Grammy. For now, she holds her breath at the suspense of its apparent indecision (will it or won't it?). Its name is just another detail my mother would likely forget when she flies away from here, one day soon, for good. Will she, won't she—today, tomorrow? Holding on hard, with fists clenched against inevitable winter, Grammy isn't saying.

Harvest time, Deb Paulson's Connecticut garden, *Photograph © Jane Booth*

*Iris pâle.*            *Iris pallida.*

P. J. Redouté. _ 59.               Victor.

# Ashes to
# Ashes

*by Domenica Di Piazza*

Author Domenica Di Piazza plants an iris garden

in memory of her mother in her essay "Ashes to Ashes."

Di Piazza is a managing editor with Lerner Publishing Group in

Minneapolis, Minnesota, where she lives and gardens. Her previously

published works include nonfiction titles for young readers. This is her

first published essay.

*For my sister, who accompanied me
into the deep end.*

*Opposite: Iris pâle, P.J. Redoute_59*

Japanese Iris
Gekka-No-Nami,
*Burpee's Bulbs & Seeds*
catalog, 1917

My sister, brother, and I cremated our mother on a sunny December afternoon. We remained silent on the drive from the city to the crematorium in rural Wisconsin, where the rubble of dried-up cornstalks lay exposed across miles of brown fields. Our mother had committed suicide the week before, placing the barrel of a revolver in her mouth and pulling the trigger. In cremating her, we were carrying out her wishes, expressed in a letter to the three of us years before.

Among her few requests, she had asked that we return her ashes to southeastern Missouri, where she had spent her girlhood summers.

The crematorium was in a dingy garage attached to the greenhouse of a Colonial-style funeral parlor. Rays of winter sun streamed through the wall of greenhouse windows near the retort (kiln). With us to say our farewell, our families and our father—long divorced from our mother—gathered around the catafalque where my mother's body lay in its cardboard casket. My sister arranged three votive candles on top, tucking a wrapped package we had assembled the night before, with its contents of dried lavender, clippings from our hair, Missouri buckeyes, and an origami crane, into an opening of the casket. As a final offering, she lay down sprays of flowering cymbidium, tied with an embroidered satin ribbon.

Tulips and bearded irises bloom in a New England garden,
*Photograph © Richard W. Brown*

We had chosen cymbidium in memory of our mother in her glory days. She had a magical way with orchids. They bloomed and outgrew their containers as if on command, with little attention from her. When they stopped producing flowers or became too large, she simply threw them out and started over with smaller, younger plants. Yet she had no real facility in the garden, caring little for the hard labor required and ignoring simple rules of symmetry. Invariably she placed short bushy specimens out of sight behind tall flowering varieties, which, when they toppled from the weight of their blooms, she neglected to stake. She paid no attention to complementary colors, choosing her plants instead for the romance of their names or for the memory of something similar her mother or her Aunt Maud had grown in their country gardens.

My orchids rarely bloom, but I carry on my mother's random, scattershot style in my own gardens. A difference is that, season after season, I labor in my plots. For reasons that are murky, even to me, I reject the advantages of modern gardening and water by hand with an old tin watering can, haul mulch in a wheelbarrow with a flat tire, and plant bulbs on my knees every fall without the cushioned comfort of a steel-framed kneeling pad.

In the autumn before my mother's death, I had planted a selection of late-blooming French tulips in soft shades of pink, apricot, and pale yellow. With the darkness of winter and the gloom that descended after her suicide, I forgot about the bulbs. Spring came early to remind me. The snow and ice melted rapidly, revealing layers of leafy mulch, and on a March morning, I headed out to relieve the bulbs of their burden. The top layers, dry and light, came away easily. As I penetrated the lowest stratum, the task required more effort. The mulch there was tightly packed and sodden, small ice crystals still clinging to the veins of the leaves. Yet I saw that the bulbs themselves had done much of the labor for me, most of them punching their way through the heavy wet leaves on their journey to the sunlight above.

My mother had talked of suicide as long as I can remember, describing it as a friend who came to call at regular, if unanticipated, intervals. I never believed this engagement of hers to be serious. I had always interpreted it as a casual flirtation with the idea of death, wielded as often as not to produce certain effects among those closest to her. I had assumed she could simply will away her friend when she tired of him and get back to the business of living. So when she finally pulled the trigger, I was stunned, like a jilted spouse, who, too late, puts together the years of clues and not-so-subtle hints that confirm a lengthy love affair.

After my mother's suicide, I understood that death had seduced her, carrying her away in its violent and powerful clutches. I could no longer deny death's allure for her. I wondered for months afterward, and still sometimes even now, if I had betrayed my mother, not only through my callous ignorance but in the reality of surviving her.

On that March morning in my garden, witness to the bulbs' upheaval, I realized that life, too, is powerful and violent. Like my

Siberian irises, misty Northeastern garden, *Photograph by Richard W. Brown*

mother in the maw of death, I, in living, was caught in the clutches of an equivalent force. Individual will was irrelevant.

Soon thereafter, in May, the tall, elegant tulips opened their petals among the greening rose bushes of my bulb garden, and I thought of the fragrance of lavender, which I would add to the garden in the coming weeks. For my birthday the next month, friends drove me into the countryside to an iris farm. We wandered among the display gardens, interplanted with peonies, taking notes on the cultivars we liked best. I had decided to create a garden of bearded iris in memory of my mother.

The year before her death, my mother had planted a small iris garden of her own. A downstairs neighbor had ripped up the front lawn to put in an abundance of vegetables, herbs, and prairie plants, mulching generously with fragrant cacao-bean hulls. Offered a corner of the garden, my mother had planted a cluster of dark purple Eleanor Roosevelt irises. She had come upon them by chance at the weekly farmers' market and, as a longtime admirer of First Lady Roosevelt, had fallen under their spell. In her usual manner, she had dug orange-pink coral bells into the center of the cluster, hiding their delicate spikes from view.

At the iris farm, I searched for those same Eleanor Roosevelt irises and came upon them in one of the plots farthest from the gravel road leading into the farm. On my notepad, I jotted down their name and location as well as those of irises of contrasting purples to plant with the Eleanor irises. We placed our orders, for late summer delivery, and drove back to the city.

When the irises arrived in September, I prepared a bed for them in the front

*Iris Pallida, The Illustrated Dictionary of Gardening,* circa 1900

246

garden. I dug up a withering shrub, attacking the chore with hand tools and digging away at the large, knotted root system with a shovel. An elderly neighbor walked past as I tugged at the roots. He looked distressed by my efforts, assuring me that, had he been younger, he would certainly have helped. Shortly afterward, as he continued on his way, the root system yielded, and I held it up for an invisible audience. "I did it!" I exclaimed.

The next day, I worked the soil, turning it over and adding peat moss for aeration in very unscientific proportions. I arranged the iris rhizomes in semicircles, avoiding a tendency to make straight, even rows and leaving room in front for coral bells to provide prominent contrast of shape and color. The physical labor completed, I went inside. My mother's ashes rest next to the fireplace, awaiting the day when my siblings and I can come together to scatter them over the hardscrabble Missouri soil.

I dipped a cup into the dark ashes, admired the light film of dust that rose into the air, and walked back to the iris garden, where I turned my mother's ashes into the earth, the sun playing off their edges in a sparkling display of silvery effervescence.

German Bearded *Iris Momauguin* and Siberian Iris Caesar's Brother, garden of Marcia Kindlmann, Killingworth, Connecticut, *Photograph © Jane Booth*

# Listening to
# My Garden

*by Kathie Bailey*

Kathie Bailey has evolved from a neglecter of houseplants to a dedicated gardener. A favorite triumph was growing foot-long sweet potatoes in Minnesota. Her current passion is reclaiming lawn areas with native plant species. In her essay "Listening to My Garden," Bailey learns a valuable lesson from her garden.

*Opposite:* A Peaceful Respite, *Photograph* © *Richard Felber*

Maybe my garden can teach me how to live.

In early April, after a week of temperatures in the 70s and 80s, I am torn. As usual I glory in the return of color to the land: the yellow of quickening willow branches, the grass greening up, the peachy glow of blossoms on the maples. I delight in the renewal of spring, smelling the earth, seeing bugs—even butterflies, the softer blue skies, evenings warm enough to stroll wearing a T-shirt.

But this year, my joy is mixed with dread and tears. I see some of the new green shoots shriveling and browning in the unseasonable heat. More of our usually hardy spring bulbs have failed to push up through the soil this year. The winter days of bitter cold without snow cover have taken their toll. I notice the juncos moving farther north, and the robins, redwings, and mallards appearing weeks earlier than ever before. Spring weather disasters, tornadoes in Iowa and Tennessee, have already begun. Our prairie smoke (a native plant with blooms resembling pink troll-doll hair) has buds, an event that usually occurs in May. Tonight I even pulled up a few sprouts of crabgrass.

I'm no fool. I've read the climate studies and projections for the future. I have an idea of what we all may be in for in the coming years. Rapidly increasing "normal" temperatures in Minnesota. Heat waves so intense that it will be unsafe to be outside. Frequent and long-lasting drought. Continued acute weather-caused disasters. Escalating wars over oil fields. Unaffordable gasoline. Life without petroleum products, including plastic. All too frightening to give more than a passing thought.

Driving my car with the air conditioning on, seeing the fragile, white blossoms open on the magnolia trees much too early, I weep.

How will I be able to garden this year at all? I am still suffering from whiplash after a car accident last September. Just when my neck and shoulder pain eases up and I can do a little more, something happens to set it off again. The pain actually seems to be getting worse. I'm not able to carry more than a few pounds at a time, and bending over from the waist to garden, with my neck angled back is definitely out! Thank God, our neighbors want to cultivate the part of our yard we share as a vegetable garden again this year. Also thank God, the friend we pay to do heavy landscaping work is available again this spring.

## Whiplash injury: *Injury resulting from a sudden sharp whipping movement of the neck and head (as of a person in a vehicle that is struck head-on or from the rear by another vehicle).*

*—Webster's Universal Encyclopedic Dictionary*

In a whiplash injury, the head and neck are thrown back when there is a sudden strong change in momentum. Maybe we are all suffering from whiplash—the plants, creatures, humans—doing our best to adapt to the change in momentum in the climate and sustaining some injuries. In fact, I feel the car accident was to some degree caused by a sudden change in the momentum of my life. It occurred at a time of increased anxiety, during a career shift.

After working as a psychotherapist for many years, I decided to incorporate my love of the arts into my work. I developed groups and workshops on creativity and expressive arts therapy. In the groups spontaneous painting, writing, movement and dance, and simple dramatic techniques are used to promote personal growth and healing. This work can affect people in profound ways—enhancing creativity, relieving stress, improving relationships, and helping people to form more authentic life paths.

It is ironic that the whiplash has stopped me from painting, writing, playing an instrument, and dancing. Here I am, helping others to do what I now cannot do myself (temporarily I hope). I miss my own forms of creative expression. Also, planting the seeds of my new work has involved some financial uncertainty, significantly more time and energy, public visibility, and increased physical demands. All these things add stress, taking a toll on my injured neck.

How can I adapt? As I contemplate a painting of an orchard I began last year and have brought out to finish now, my mind's eye sees hands reaching down from the tree branches, reaching to help. I have a sense that there are sources of help during these hard times. Nature is one of them. For me, nature has always been an inexhaustible source of relaxation and well-being. Spending time outside restores my connection with my deep inner center, so that I am more available to myself and other people. I'm hoping nature can also help me adapt to changes in the world.

More than half our yard is now planted with species native to our area of Minnesota. The transformation began about ten years ago when the city doubled the size of our yard by narrowing the street in front of our house. We decided to turn the new land into a native prairie garden instead of having the city cover it with sod. I had been reading Sara Stein's *Noah's Garden* and *Planting Noah's Garden*, two delightfully written books on the extensive environmental damage caused by the standard lawn and flower garden, and the benefits of replacing them with native species. According to Stein, lawns are one of the most significant causes of environmental damage in the United States.

Lawns are composed of grasses that originated in Europe or Africa and are alien to U.S. ecosystems. Besides requiring excessive water and poisonous chemicals to thrive, lawn grasses form a thick mat which effectively seals off water from penetrating beneath it. Instead of allowing the water to be absorbed into the earth, it runs off, carrying polluting chemicals with it. The native plants have evolved together with microorganisms, insects, birds, and animals, providing the perfect food and habitat to support the ecosystem we all depend on for life. Lawns replace huge areas of native ecosystems across the country, effectively starving out and killing off native species.

With inspiration from my partner and free plants from a neighbor, who is a well-known developer specializing in native gardens, we got started. After seeing the wonderful results, we've converted more and more of the lawn to native plantings.

Since our native garden has matured, we have large clusters of migrating monarch butterflies fluttering around our yard for weeks in the fall. Bright goldfinches perch on the taller plants. Hummingbirds stop over on their way south. In the morning we open the shades to a sunlit meadow alive with birds and dragonflies. Our hedgerow is home to rabbits, chipmunks, and squirrels. In the winter, tall golden grasses and interesting seedheads form sculptures above the snow.

The garden soil was originally hardpacked clay and gravel covered by 2 to 3 inches of topsoil. After about three years, the soil was 6 to 8 inches deep; rich, dark, and crumbly. How could this have happened? The prairie plants have deep root systems that bring minerals up from the subsoil, fertilizing and enriching the topsoil. The microorganisms and underground grubs and insects the native plants attract recycle the soil through their bodies, breaking it up and adding even more nutrients. By following nature's pattern, we have created a nourishing environment, full of beauty and life-giving variety.

With the climatic shift, the native plants are faring much better than their hybrid cousins. Over the last few years of changed winters, all of our hundreds of bulbs, except a few crocus, have stopped coming up. The buddleia has died. Hostas have dried out. Other domesticated garden plants have been unable to withstand the cold without snow cover.

But the natives are doing fine. They are surviving, even flourishing in the hard winters and hotter summers. Evolved over millennia of intense heat, deep cold, drought, and flood, they have developed resilience. Their roots twine together deep underground to form a complex mat that holds the soil in a tight grip, retaining moisture and retarding erosion. I think I'll follow their lead. What is my garden telling me?

> Let what no longer fits my life die a natural death.
> Grow only at the pace my structure can support.
> Stay close to the earth.
> Connect with my natural community of friends, neighbors, and family.
> Deepen my roots.

I lie back and rest in the evening, the open window letting a cool breeze flow into my too-warm house. Winding down after another week of too much—too many new projects all at once, too much work, too many ideas, too much thinking and worrying, all taking a toll on my neck. Parts of my head actually hurt just to touch. What is this? Am I developing some strange disease?

I try to relax, remembering what a friend shared at the Passover Seder the night before: The ancient physical attitude of prayer among Middle Eastern peoples is to hold out the hands with palms up, cupped to receive. I try it while lying down. How trusting this feels. I wish I could just relax and simply receive the beauty of spring's arrival. It pains me that I can't. Instead, my impulse is to shut down, to stop feeling. Opening to the beauty is to open also to the pain, the woundedness of the earth. But in shutting down I lose connection. It's like shutting the door on love because it makes me feel vulnerable to being hurt.

I try to untangle the knot in my mind and my neck. I ask, What do I need to do to heal this chronic pain and limitation? From somewhere inside me a voice answers, "Go back." Go back? But I do know what it means. Go back to the deeper roots of myself, to paying attention to my emotions and natural rhythms. Slow down, stop forcing the growth. Listen.

I cry a few more tears, and the pain in my head eases a little. From deep in my belly, a darkness seems to rise up, spreading into the atmosphere around me. The darkness is a deep, deep blue, reminding me of the color of the sky at night. It is an ancient part of me emerging, seeking a place in my life. Its depths feel calming, peaceful. I look out the window. It is dusk. The pale new leaves glow just as if it were the first spring on earth.

Tranquil Japanese garden, the grounds of the family home of
Sir Winston Churchill in Chartwell, Kent, UK., *Photograph © Dixie Cornell*